11

8

12

5   13

14   22
      2120

6

19   15   16

23

10

17   17

18

9

12 London, England—rejected by ATS; later US code clerk during Blitz (1940); after Pyrenees escape (1943); after Madrid (1943)

13 Metz, France area—ambulance driver **near Maginot Line** (1940)

14 Loire Valley—ambulance driver (1940)

15 Vichy, France—first SOE mission, Operation Geologist 5 (1941)

16 Lyon, France—Heckler Circuit (1941)

17 Perpignan, France across **Pyrenees** to **San Juan de las Abadesas, Spain**—(1942)

18 Madrid, Spain—SOE agent with cover as *Chicago Times* journalist (1943)

19 La Creuse, France—**Maidou-sur-Crozant** in central France, SOE agent disguised as peasant (1944)

20 Cosne-sur-Loire, Nièvre—5 hours SE of Paris—essential Maquis trainer and organizer (1944)

21 Sury-en-Vaux, Cher—disguised as peasant goat herder, invaluable spy in German infested region (1944)

22 Sury-es-Bois, Cher—trained resistance fighters, organized weapons, money, supply air drops (1944)

23 Le Chambon-sur-Lignon, Haute-Loire—dropped peasant garb, provided invaluable communications, deliveries, commanded 5 companies of 400 men for sabotage missions; lived with Fayol and wife, and bestowed title La Madone by her loyal Maquis soldiers (1944)

24 Barnesville, MD—Virginia and Paul move to their farm (1959)

THE MYSTERIOUS VIRGINIA HALL

THE MYSTERIOUS
VIRGINIA
HALL

WORLD WAR II's
MOST DANGEROUS SPY

CLAUDIA FRIDDELL

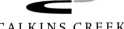

CALKINS CREEK
AN IMPRINT OF ASTRA BOOKS FOR YOUNG READERS
New York

For information about permission to reproduce selections from this book,
please contact permissions@astrapublishinghouse.com.

Calkins Creek
An imprint of Astra Books for Young Readers,
a division of Astra Publishing House
astrapublishinghouse.com

Printed in China

The Library of Congress Cataloging-in-Publication Data is available upon request.
Library of Congress Control Number: 2024017678

ISBN: 978-1-6626-8059-5 (hc)
ISBN: 978-1-6626-8060-1 (eBook)

First edition

10 9 8 7 6 5 4 3 2 1

Design by Red Herring Design
The text is set in Rockwell.
The titles are set in Aku & Kamu.

TO

VIRGINIA HALL'S FAMILY
and my fearless leader,
CAROLYN YODER—*CF*

CONTENTS

FOREWORD

Please note before I begin that Virginia Hall's family and friends called her by her nickname, "Dindy," and I invite you to do the same.

As a kid in the '70s, I remember the blank expression on my friend's face when I told him about my great-aunt Dindy. "She was a spy with a wooden leg who shot herself in the foot while hunting birds in a Turkish swamp, and she dressed up like an old maid in World War II, and sold cheese to the Germans soldiers, and stole their secrets because they didn't know she spoke German and . . ." No response. I think I could have told him that my great-aunt was an octopus, and his reaction would have been the same. In a way, Dindy was a conversation-stopper back then, but now I understand why. She was simply the first of her kind.

Dindy somehow managed to live the equivalent of twenty regular-size lives and spent most of it trying to save the world from, as she put it, "the usual enemies of the civilized world." And somehow, author Claudia Friddell has managed to tell Dindy's massive life story in photographs and a crystal-clear voice that sets each scene precisely and makes the reader feel like they are there. For most of the book, I felt like a fly on the wall in a wartime French café.

Fortunately for us, Dindy was not the last of her kind. Over the years, I have had the pleasure to meet several dozen retired female CIA agents at events honoring my great-aunt. They all knew Dindy's story backward and forward, and every one of them had that same eagle-like fire in their eyes, and no doubt each was perfectly capable of winning a car chase and a bar fight, any day of the week. Just like Dindy.

Early in Claudia's book, I found myself saying "Wow!" after nearly every page. How was this possible? I have heard (and told) Dindy's story hundreds of times, but this book made the story feel fresh and new. After I finished *The Mysterious Virginia Hall*, I realized that I had been taken on a worldwide, magic carpet-like journey with a hundred mind-boggling stops along the way. My advice, dear reader, is to board this magic carpet but to fly it slowly. There is so much to see, and you won't want to miss a thing!

Finally, I would like to congratulate Claudia, a Baltimore girl, just like Dindy. *The Mysterious Virginia Hall* is a truly wonderful book. I am also thankful for the care and respect Claudia gave to Dindy's niece, my mother, Lorna Catling, whose eyes always sparkle with excitement and pride whenever she tells Dindy's story and shares her album of black-and-white photos, many of which you will enjoy in the coming pages.

Bradford D. S. Catling
Virginia Hall's great-nephew

DINDY

Virginia Hall
might have been the name
on her birth certificate,
but thanks to a nickname
from her brother, John,
Dindy was the name that stuck.

Most young girls
of Baltimore society a century ago
were expected to follow
in their mothers' ladylike footsteps—
but Dindy made
a path of her own.

1911. Dindy and her older brother, John, had a
happy, active childhood together at Boxhorn Farm in
Maryland. She called him "Johnny" and he gave his
sister the nickname "Dindy" by mispronouncing her
original nickname "Ginger."

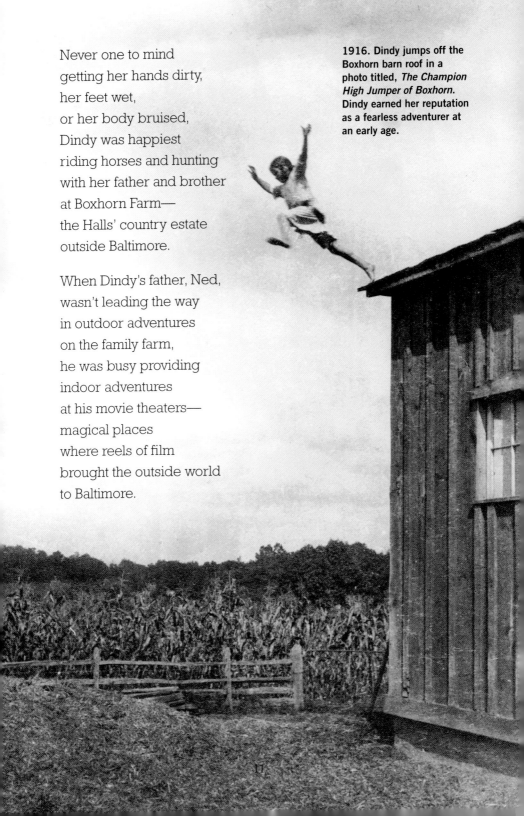

Never one to mind
getting her hands dirty,
her feet wet,
or her body bruised,
Dindy was happiest
riding horses and hunting
with her father and brother
at Boxhorn Farm—
the Halls' country estate
outside Baltimore.

When Dindy's father, Ned,
wasn't leading the way
in outdoor adventures
on the family farm,
he was busy providing
indoor adventures
at his movie theaters—
magical places
where reels of film
brought the outside world
to Baltimore.

1916. Dindy jumps off the Boxhorn barn roof in a photo titled, *The Champion High Jumper of Boxhorn*. Dindy earned her reputation as a fearless adventurer at an early age.

For generations
the Halls had been
fascinated by cultures
vastly different and worlds away
from Maryland shores.

At the age of nine,
Dindy's grandfather stowed away
on his sea captain father's clipper ship,
and later captained a ship of his own
that brought Asian goods to America.

While many of their friends
crossed the Chesapeake Bay
for seaside vacations,
Dindy's family
crossed the Atlantic Ocean
for European adventures.

From her very first
transatlantic voyage
at the age of four,
Dindy stowed away
a love for Europe.

1910. Four-year-old Dindy looks
upward from a ship's deck on her
first of many voyages to Europe.
The Halls were headed for the
Brussels International Exposition.
Their love for intercontinental
travel no doubt influenced Dindy's
determination to become a US
ambassador.

When Dindy wasn't chasing
after her brother
at Boxhorn Farm,
or exploring foreign countries
with her family,
she was blazing
her own unique trail
at Roland Park Country School—
an all-girls school in Baltimore.

Never once
in twelve years at RPCS
did she hear—
You can't do that, you're a girl!
Because, unlike in the outside world,
every club and team
at Dindy's school
was not only made up of girls—
they were all *led* by girls.
Nicknamed the *Fighting Blade*
by her ninth-grade classmates,
Dindy was a natural leader
in sports, student government,
and school activities.
She was often
her own harshest critic,
but her devoted classmates
gave her an endearing tribute
on her yearbook senior page:

She is, by her own confession,
cantankerous and capricious,
but in spite of it all
we would not do without her;
for she is our class-president,
the editor-in-chief of this book,
and one of the mainstays
of the basket-ball and hockey teams.
She has been acclaimed
the most original of our class,
and she lives up
to her reputation
at all times.
The one thing to expect from Dind
is the unexpected.

It was certainly unexpected
the day Dindy
surprised her classmates
by wearing a favorite
new bracelet to school—
a live, slithering garter snake
coiled around her wrist.

Dindy, inspired by Shakespeare's play,
As You Like It, made it clear
on her senior page
just how much
she valued her independence
when she stated

I must have liberty, withal as large a charter as I please.

1924. Dindy, on right, loved theater and often played male parts in her all-girls school plays. A hint of her indomitable spirit is reflected on her Roland Park Country School senior page: "Though professing to hold Man in contempt, Dindy is yet his closest counterpart—in costume."

Dindy had no way
of knowing then
of the bold sacrifices
she would later make
to prove her own independence—
or the extraordinary risks
she would take
to defend and preserve
liberty for so many others.

Mr. Hall encouraged his daughter's
independent nature,
and while Mrs. Hall
accepted Dindy's free spirit,
she still expected
her beautiful, bright,
and accomplished daughter
to join the path
of other young ladies
of Baltimore society
by marrying a worthy husband
and starting a family nearby.

But in 1920, when Dindy was fourteen,
a family visit to London's American embassy
dashed Barbara Hall's dreams for her daughter
and steered Dindy toward a different path—
one that didn't include
a husband, a family, or a home in Maryland.

Once she learned
American ambassadors
represented the United States
in foreign countries,
Dindy decided this was her destiny.

She wasn't the least bit discouraged
when her father explained
there were no female ambassadors—
it only fueled Dindy's determination.

After all, being a girl
had never gotten in the way
of her dreams before.

A maverick at home and at school,
Dindy was ready
to take her first step
toward a future
most women didn't want
and couldn't get
in the 1920s—
an overseas job in the United States Foreign Service.

With her father's blessing,
and her mother's disapproval,
Roland Park's *most original* student
set off on a most unexpected journey,
leaving her hometown
and her nickname behind.

VIRGINIA

If Virginia was going to be an ambassador,
she had a lot to learn.
Virginia attended Radcliffe and Barnard,
two of America's top colleges
available to women,
but she had become frustrated
by what she described as
a lot of uninteresting required courses.
After a year at each school
she craved more worldly opportunities.

So in 1926, at the age of twenty,
Virginia crossed the Atlantic—
this time without her family—
to study languages
and economics in Paris
at the École Libre des Sciences Politiques.

1926. American-born Josephine Baker— Black singer, dancer, and actress during the Jazz Age. Like Virginia, the famous entertainer became a spy to aid her beloved France in fighting fascism during World War II. She gathered intelligence, smuggled documents, and hid Jewish refugees, resistance fighters, and weapons.

What a remarkable time
for a young, independent-minded
woman like Virginia to live in Paris—
a city bursting with the creative energy
of innovative artists, writers, and entertainers
like Pablo Picasso, Ernest Hemingway, and Josephine Baker.

The 1920s in France
was a decade so rich in culture,
an era so full of free expression,
it was called *Les Années Folles*—the Crazy Years.

Living on her own,
free to dress as she liked
and act as she pleased,
Virginia found
her independence in France—
the place she now called
her second homeland.

From Paris
Virginia headed to Vienna, Austria,
where she continued her studies
in languages and economics
at the Consular Academy.
Virginia strengthened her French language skills
and expanded her knowledge
of French culture and geography
by taking summer courses in Toulouse,
Grenoble, and Strasbourg.
She never perfected her French accent,
but her love for France and its people grew.

1928. After studying in Paris,
22-year-old Virginia, seated
in the middle, enjoyed Vienna
where she earned her college
degree at the Consular Academy.

After three years of adventures in Europe,
Virginia returned to America
with a college degree
from the Consular Academy.
Focused on preparing herself
for a career as a foreign service officer
in the US State Department,
Virginia started a year of graduate studies
in French and economics
at George Washington University
in the nation's capital.

But Virginia's focus was jolted
when the stock market crashed
in the fall of 1929.
The Great Depression followed,
devastating the entire country.
Jobs were lost, bank accounts were emptied,
and food became scarce.

Along with millions of Americans,
the Halls' way of life changed forever.
Virginia's brother lost his job,
and her father scrambled to keep
his businesses in operation.

Despite the hardships
caused by the Depression,
Virginia completed her graduate studies
and was ready to take the next step
toward a future in diplomacy.

Even though only six of the fifteen hundred
foreign service officers at that time were women,

Virginia was confident
that with her extensive education,
travel experience, and language skills,
she would easily pass
the Foreign Service entrance exam.

But Virginia misjudged its difficulty.
Her perfect oral foreign language proficiency score
did not make up for her poor performance
on the more subjective oral portion
and the challenging written test.
In December 1929, Virginia failed the exam.

Rejected but not defeated,
Virginia was determined to prove
she was just as capable as any man
to serve as a diplomat,
so she retook the exam
the following July.
Despite an improvement
on her written tests,
She had failed again.

Virginia told a friend her only path
to a job in the Foreign Service
was through the back door.
That meant she would need to apply
to the State Department
for consular clerk positions—
secretarial jobs—
in foreign embassies.

Unfortunately, tragic circumstances
would put a hold on her diplomatic dreams.

Virginia was raised
to shrug off discomfort
and tackle challenges head on—
but she and her family
reeled from shock
when her beloved father
died of a heart attack
in the winter of 1931.

Virginia couldn't imagine
a world without her father—
her biggest fan.
He had always been there to encourage
his spirited daughter
to explore her own interests
and follow her own dreams.

Virginia and her brother rallied together
to help their mother
adjust to a new life
without her loving husband.
Once John moved his family
into Boxhorn Farm
to help with expenses,
Virginia was ready
to renew her pursuit
of a future in the Foreign Service.

While most of her friends
were getting married
and starting families in Baltimore,
Virginia was applying
for clerk positions
in foreign embassies.

In the summer of 1931,
twenty-five-year-old Virginia
received her first job offer,
which she accepted without hesitation.
Ready to embark on a new adventure,
Virginia headed to the American embassy
in Warsaw, Poland.

1931. After helping her family adjust after the
Depression and her father's death, Virginia took
her first post as a consular clerk at the American
embassy in Warsaw, Poland. Although she found the
secretarial work boring, she did learn the valuable
spy skill of coding and decoding telegrams.

Starting at the bottom
of the State Department ladder
was not in Virginia's plans,
but if doing secretarial tasks
was her only path to promotion
in the Foreign Service,
she was ready to get to work—
no matter how tedious
the work might be.

Living in Warsaw, however,
was far from dull.
Poland was in a precarious position
pressed between the Soviet Union and Germany—
two countries ruled by dictators
plotting to overthrow peaceful democracies.

Adolf Hitler in Germany
and Joseph Stalin in the Soviet Union
were busy building armies,
spreading propaganda,
and stoking violent mobs
to incite fear among the masses
while they prepared
to invade neighboring countries.

Virginia saw firsthand
how the Polish people suffered
as turmoil spread
throughout the country.

She desperately wanted to help,
but there was little she could do as a clerk.
So in September of 1932,
Virginia completed the written
portion of the Foreign Service exam
and then waited for weeks
for the oral questions
to come in the mail.

They never arrived.

Frustrated by another missed chance
to join the Foreign Service,
and eager for a more challenging job,
Virginia applied for a transfer.

In the spring of 1933, Virginia arrived
at the American consulate in Izmir, Turkey,
hoping for more responsibility as a clerk.

While disappointed that her job
was more of the same
tedious secretarial tasks,
Virginia was at least happy
to find herself
near the salt marshes
of the Gediz Peninsula—
a bird hunter's paradise.

One clear December morning,
with four friends by her side
and her father's shotgun in hand,
Virginia set out
for a day of snipe hunting.
She had missed hunting
at Boxhorn Farm
and was ready for the challenge
of pursuing this small,
elusive marsh bird—
but nothing prepared Virginia
for a fateful climb over a wire fence.

1923. Seventeen-year-old Dindy holds a
shotgun in one hand and a dove in the
other after hunting at Boxhorn Farm. She
carried a hunting license in most of the
countries she visited before the war.

It all happened in an instant.
Her foot slipped.
Her gun dropped.
Virginia reached for it, and

BANG!

Her shotgun accidentally fired,
blasting an explosion of lead pellets
into her foot.
Bones shattered and blood flowed
as Virginia fell to the ground.

Her faithful friends
tightened tourniquets
to stop the bleeding
and whispered support
to ward off shock.
With a stretcher made from hunting jackets
draped over shotguns,
they rushed Virginia through the muddy marsh
to the nearest hospital.

The doctors in Izmir acted just as quickly,
and it seemed she would be back on her feet again soon.
But Virginia's left foot
turned from blue to black.
She couldn't shake
the deadly infection of gangrene.

Dr. Lorrin Shepard,
the head of the American Hospital in Istanbul,
rushed to Virginia's rescue.

Penicillin—the antibiotic
that could stop the infection
from spreading throughout her body—
had been discovered,
but it was not yet available for patient use.
There was only one option
to save Virginia's life.

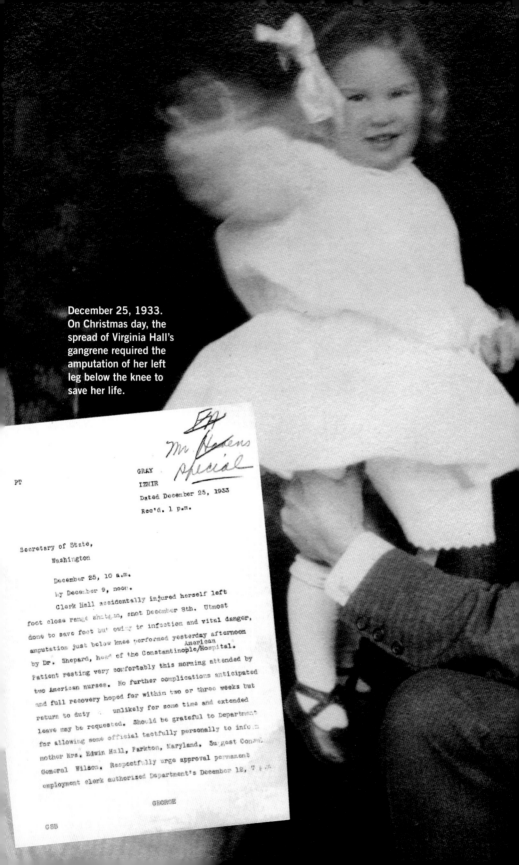

December 25, 1933. On Christmas day, the spread of Virginia Hall's gangrene required the amputation of her left leg below the knee to save her life.

PT

GRAY
IZMIR

Dated December 25, 1933
Rec'd. 1 p.m.

Secretary of State,
Washington

December 25, 10 a.m.

My December 9, noon.

Clerk Hall accidentally injured herself left foot close range shotgun, shot December 9th. Utmost done to save foot but owing to infection and vital danger, amputation just below knee performed yesterday afternoon by Dr. Shepard, head of the Constantinople/American Hospital. Patient resting very comfortably this morning attended by two American nurses. No further complications anticipated and full recovery hoped for within two or three weeks but return to duty unlikely for some time and extended leave may be requested. Should be grateful to Department for allowing some official tactfully personally to inform mother Mrs. Edwin Hall, Parkton, Maryland. Suggest Consul General Wilson. Respectfully urge approval permanent employment clerk authorized Department's December 12, 7 p.m.

GEORGE

CSB

On Christmas Day in 1933,
Dr. Shepard amputated
Virginia's left leg
just below her knee.

Until now Virginia's greatest loss
had been her beloved father.
Delirious from the unbearable pain
and the loss of blood,
Virginia dreamed
of his arms wrapped around her.
She dreamed of him
rocking her in his lap,
whispering that she needed
to be strong for her mother.

Dindy's father promised
he would come back for her
if the pain was too much.
But he also knew she was a fighter,
and he hoped she would stay
and keep up the fight.

Virginia may have lost her leg that day,
but she held tight to that dream
for the rest of her life.

1908. Dindy adored her father who had indulged her
adventurous spirit and love for male-oriented activities.
She rarely spoke of the suffering she endured due
to her hunting accident, and was not particularly
religious, but she did share with her family vivid
memories of her deceased father appearing at her
hospital bedside after her amputation, urging her to
hang on to life.

VIRGINIA AND CUTHBERT

After she gained enough strength,
Virginia returned home to Boxhorn Farm.

At the same place
she ran free as a child,
Virginia recovered
from painful leg surgeries
to prevent infection.

At the same place
she learned to hunt, fish,
and ride a horse,
she learned to walk all over again—
this time dragging along
seven pounds of wood, leather, and metal.

Virginia not only enjoyed idyllic childhood summers riding horses, hunting, raising animals, and exploring the 110-acres of Boxhorn Farm—she also returned to her family home after her amputation to regain her strength and relearn to walk with a prothesis, which she named *Cuthbert*.

Every day Virginia strapped on
her prosthetic leg,
a new constant companion
she named *Cuthbert*.
She attached the wooden leg
to a leather corset,
which she then strapped
to a belt wrapped around her waist.
To protect her skin
from the endless rubbing
against Cuthbert,
Virginia fitted a woolen sock
around her stump.

At the bottom
of Virginia's wooden leg
was a flexible joint
that connected to a rubber-soled metal foot
she called her *aluminum puppy.*
While the metal joint
gave her the flexibility of an ankle,
without nerve endings
she couldn't feel
the ground beneath her.
So, with practice,
Virginia learned to move her leg
with a slight swing of her hip.

Used to vigorous sporting challenges growing up,
Virginia remained disciplined
with her recovery routines
to regain strength and balance.

After months of surgeries and therapy,
Virginia no longer needed crutches or cane.
She and Cuthbert
were ready to step back into the world.

In 1934, less than a year after her accident,
Virginia was not only steady on her feet,
she was heading back to Europe—
this time as a clerk
at the American consulate in Venice, Italy.

Often working seven days a week,
Virginia proved she could handle
greater responsibilities
than secretarial jobs.
The vice consul even trusted her
to fill in when he was out of town.

Virginia faced greater physical challenges
outside the consulate while navigating
the bumpy cobblestone streets,
steep steps, and bridges of Venice.
Always the problem solver,
Virginia found the perfect solution
to ease the burden on Cuthbert—
she bought a gondola
and hired a boatman named Angelo
to coach her through Venice's canals.

1936. With the guidance of
her rowing coach, Virginia
braces herself with her
prosthetic left leg for stability
as she learns to steer her own
gondola through the canals of
Venice, Italy. The inscription
on the back of the photo
reads, *Angelo is beginning to
be proud of my rowing
but what a backache!*

While she gained responsibility
at the consulate in Venice,
Virginia grew increasingly concerned
by the political turmoil in Europe.
America wasn't the only country
devastated by the stock market crash in 1929.

Throughout the 1930s,
European countries that had depended
on US economic support
to rebuild from the destruction
of the First World War
suffered a catastrophic depression
of their own.

Vicious dictators seized on the hopelessness
of millions of unemployed and starving Europeans
by promising them jobs and a brighter future.

In Italy, Virginia was disgusted
by the rising popularity
of Benito Mussolini—
a brutal dictator whose fascist ideology
of Italian superiority
and authoritarian control
encouraged military violence
against anyone who opposed his oppressive laws.

1940. Adolf Hitler poses
in front of the Eiffel Tower
on his only visit to Paris
after the city surrendered
to Germany in June.

Italians weren't the only Europeans
losing their individual freedoms
to fascist dictators.
Millions of unemployed and hungry Germans
were clinging desperately
to the promises and lies
of another rising dictator, Adolf Hitler,
the leader of the fascist Nazi Party.

Hitler declared that the Germanic Aryans,
whom Nazis believed to be the master race,
were superior to all others.

This laid the foundation
for placing the blame
and naming scapegoats
for Germany's unemployment and poverty.

With the guise of national pride and patriotism,
Hitler promoted fear and hate
toward anyone who was not German
and anyone he considered
different or dangerous.

Hitler led a reign of terror
ordering his Nazi soldiers
to lock up, torture, and kill
homosexuals, the disabled,
and all those who disagreed
with his political beliefs.

But no group was in more danger
from his maniacal hatred than Jews—
his scapegoats for Germany's problems.

Virginia was horrified by the growing abuses
against her Jewish friends and neighbors.
She knew there was little she could do as a clerk
to help freedom prevail,
so she made plans once again
to take the entrance exam.
Because she had worked
in the Foreign Service
for more than five years,
she was no longer required
to take the written tests.
She now only needed to pass
the oral interview.

Confident that this time she would succeed,
Virginia mailed in her application.
She never dreamed that this time,
Cuthbert would be the one
to stand in her way.

DENIED!

Virginia was shocked and confused
when she read her rejection
from the State Department—

The regulation governing physical examinations
to the Foreign Services prescribe that
amputation of any portion of a limb,
except fingers or toes . . .
is a cause for rejection,
and it would not be possible for Miss Hall
to qualify for entry into the Service
under these regulations.

Hadn't she proven
to everyone who knew her
that a mere amputation
hadn't gotten in her way?

Virginia sent back an appeal.
A family friend even wrote a letter
to President Franklin D. Roosevelt
on her behalf.

Hadn't President Roosevelt shown the world
that crippling polio didn't get in *his* way?

1924. Franklin Delano Roosevelt was diagnosed with crippling polio in 1921 at the age of thirty-nine. Undeterred by the resulting paralysis in his legs, Roosevelt was elected governor of the state of New York in 1928 and President of the United States in 1932. He served two extra terms to lead the country during World War II. Despite President Roosevelt's advocacy for Virginia Hall and other applicants with disabilities for the State Department, she was denied promotion.

Surely the president
would admire her gumption
and welcome her services.
As it turned out,
Roosevelt did share his disapproval
of Virginia's rejection
based on her disability
with his secretary of state, Cordell Hull—

Why, Oh, Why do the regulations
governing entrance into the career service
prescribe that amputation of any portion of a limb,
except fingers or toes, disqualify the applicant?

. . . It seems to me that a regulation of this kind is a great mistake
because it might exclude a first-class applicant . . .
I have known many people with wooden legs
who dance just as well as many diplomats do who have natural legs.

Perhaps Hull was annoyed
by Virginia's campaign to fight his decision.
In his response to President Roosevelt,
Hull said that, in addition to Virginia's disability,
she wasn't qualified for the position—
despite the praise she received
from her bosses at the Venice consulate.

The president could not argue with that.
The fight was over,
and Virginia's rejection was final.

In the summer of 1938,
after a year of unsuccessful appeals,
Virginia was transferred
to a new remote post
at the consulate in Tallinn, Estonia.

After another frustrating year as a clerk,
Virginia finally faced the facts—
there was no hope for promotion,
no path to a future in the Foreign Service.

In late May of 1939,
after a decade of honing
her government and language skills
to become a diplomat for democracy,
Virginia resigned from the State Department
and returned to Paris.

But Virginia would not leave Europe.
she would not desert the countries
she had grown to love,
most especially France,
while tyrants trampled their citizens' freedoms.

1939. Seven years after Virginia first witnesses abuses toward the Poles, German troops invade and conquer Poland.

On September 1, 1939,
German troops invaded Poland,
igniting World War II.

Two days later,
Britain and France
declared war on Germany.

Still recovering
from the devastating toll
of World War I
and the Great Depression,
the United States could not afford
to enter a war
clear across the Atlantic.

America's inaction
in fighting against the spread
of fascism in Europe
while Hitler's troops advanced
on France and Britain,
infuriated Virginia.
In October, 1939,
she headed to London,
hoping to join the new women's branch
of the British Army—
the Auxiliary Territorial Service.

1938. This World War II poster urges British women to join the ATS—Auxiliary Territorial Service. Formed in 1938 as "a woman's army" to free male soldiers to serve on the front, the ATS denied Virginia Hall entry due to her American citizenship.

But when she tried to enlist,
Virginia received a
familiar response—

DENIED!

This time it wasn't a disability
that stood in her way.
It was her passport.

Only British women were
accepted for service.

Virginia returned to Paris
where she met refugees
who had fled their countries
for the safety of France.
They described atrocities
Jews were suffering from Nazi abuses.

Virginia's disgust fueled a fury inside her.
Cuthbert may have stopped her
from getting a job as an ambassador,
and her US citizenship
may have prevented her from
wearing a British uniform,
but Virginia would find a way
to help freedom prevail—
one that did not require
the approval of the State Department.

1939. Virginia sent this
postcard to her family at
Boxhorn Farm on September
3rd, the day WWII was
declared in Europe. It reads:

*And so the catastrophe
has begun. I can't begin to
express the horror I feel at
this useless slaughter, being
embarked upon, caused by
the usual enemies of the
civilized world. Everything
here is quiet. Love to all,
Virginia.*

In February, 1940,
Virginia found a way
to join the fight against the Germans
in her beloved France.

Without telling her family,
thirty-four-year-old Virginia
signed on as an ambulance driver
with France's Ninth Artillery Regiment.

After training,
Virginia headed for duty
in northeastern France
outside of Metz
where German troops
were penetrating the French border.

Without hesitation
Virginia drove into the fray,
loaded up wounded French warriors,
and carried them to safety.
Back and forth, day and night, in and out of war zones—
it was back-breaking, heartbreaking, dangerous work,
but for Virginia the risks were worth it.

Driving an army ambulance was much more rewarding
than answering letters and filing reports
in a consulate office.

While Virginia transported injured soldiers
near the Maginot Line—
a series of French concrete fortifications
built along the French and German border

to prevent a German invasion—
Hitler's troops
conquered country after country.

In April, Germany had invaded Denmark and Norway.
The following month,
Luxembourg, the Netherlands, and Belgium
all surrendered to Hitler.

Now that Hitler controlled Belgium,
a country that borders both France and Germany,
the Nazi army executed a plan that the French
assumed was impossible.
They sent a fleet of German tanks
to plow through
Belgium's dense Ardennes forests
to invade France.

The German invasion escalated the fighting
on the eastern border of France
where Virginia worked nonstop,
battling exhaustion and discomfort.

Racing across bumpy roads and fields
relentlessly pushing a clutch with her left leg
caused Cuthbert to rub her stump raw.

Dealing with Cuthbert was a constant burden,
but Virginia kept complaints
of any pain or suffering to herself.
She was grateful
to be in the thick of the fight
against the Germans—
making a difference and saving lives.

Virginia didn't fear the hardships and hazards
of driving in and out of war zones,
but she hated to worry her mother
back at Boxhorn Farm.
So in letters home,
Virginia told her mother she was
well taken care of . . . with *plenty of good food,*
hoping to put a positive spin
on her battlefield adventures.
Her mother wasn't fooled.

Mrs. Hall told a *Baltimore Sun* reporter
that her daughter's
carefully chosen words were
well intentioned, but they afford me little consolation,
for in her characteristic manner
she is trying to make things sound better for me.

Mrs. Hall knew
her daring Dindy
would never share details
of the true dangers she faced.

On June 14th, 1940,
only a month after Germany invaded France,
Paris surrendered.

This devastating defeat
ended Virginia's heroics
as an ambulance driver
and further fueled
her passion to defend France.
She was disgusted
when the new French leader, Philippe Pétain,
signed an armistice with Hitler—
an agreement giving Germany occupational control
of the north and west regions of France,
known as the occupied zone.

Pétain, once a celebrated WWI general
revered as *the lion of Verdun,*
was now a Nazi puppet
who controlled the southern two-fifths of France
called the unoccupied or free zone.
But the region was free in name only.
Pétain, a close collaborator with Hitler,
was now the leader of his own authoritarian regime
based in Vichy, France.

Virginia later recalled,
at the time of defeat
we all felt nothing but fury.
She refused to accept
that her beloved France—
the country that had aided America
in its War of Independence—
had given up its own fight.

She was ready to stand with
the French patriots
who still believed in their country's motto
from the French Revolution—
"Liberty, Equality, Fraternity."
Once Pétain took control,
he replaced it with the new Vichy slogan—
"Work, Family, Fatherland."

Virginia hated to see
the horrific transformation of Paris.
The city that was once a beacon
of tolerance and free expression
was now the occupied zone headquarters
for the oppressive Nazi regime.
Virginia felt helpless
as her friends and neighbors
suffered food shortages and curfews.
And she was enraged by the
Germans' random arrests and attacks
on the French Jews.

In August 1940,
Virginia decided to return to Britain.
Maybe there,
in the only country left
standing up to Germany,
Virginia could find
another way to help
France regain its independence.

Little did Virginia know that,
on her journey to London,
a chance meeting
with a stranger on a train
would change her life forever.

George Bellows introduced himself
as a salesman
when he first met Virginia.
He didn't know her well enough
to reveal his true occupation.

Virginia had a good sense
of whom to trust,
and she felt comfortable
sharing with Bellows
her background and her passion
for defending France's freedom.

After listening to Virginia describe
her European experiences
as a consular clerk and
a French ambulance driver,
Bellows was impressed by Virginia's
bravery, her keen observations,
and her devotion to the liberation of France.

Virginia had no idea that
Bellows was an agent for the SOE—
Britain's new Special Operations Executive spy agency.

She had no idea
he was thinking
that even though the SOE
was not yet recruiting female spies,
Virginia Hall might be just
the recruit they needed.

All Virginia knew
was that she trusted this man
when he slipped a phone number
into her hand as they parted.

When Virginia arrived in London,
she did not call Bellows's contact,
but she did take his advice
to check in at the American embassy.

Her experiences as an ambulance driver
in the thick of Nazi-occupied territory
impressed the Foreign Service officers.
She was immediately offered a job
in the US military attaché's office.

Virginia's uneventful days
as a code clerk
were overshadowed
by the terror of the Blitz—
Germany's relentless
nightly aerial bombing raids
that began in September, 1940
just two weeks after Virginia
arrived in London.
They would continue to ravage London
and other British towns and cities for eight months.

With hundreds of thousands of other civilians,
Virginia endured citywide blackouts
that darkened the Nazi targets.
Piercing sirens sent masses of residents
scampering for cover in their basements
and to underground air-raid shelters.

Virginia felt committed to joining
the fight against the Nazis,
but she also felt a pull toward home.
She decided to appease her worried mother
and make arrangements
to return to Boxhorn Farm for Christmas.

But fate would change her plans once again.

Virginia would not be home for the holidays after all.
In January, 1941,
Virginia received the news
that her passage home had only been valid
for one year after her resignation
from the State Department—
a year and a half earlier.

Without a ticket home,
Virginia decided to stay in London
and find a way to get back to France.

1940. People pack into a London underground station used as an air-raid shelter during the Blitz. Virginia lived in London during the most intensive barrage of German bombings beginning September 7, 1940.

Mighty forces against democracies
were spreading around the world
now that Italy and Japan had joined Germany
to form the Axis alliance.
The world needed Britain to hang on,
and Britain needed allies to join the fight.

Far from home,
and alone in a war zone,
Virginia decided to call the number
Bellows had given her on the train.
It belonged to Nicolas Bodington.

Soon after the New Year of 1941,
Virginia was invited
to a party at Bodington's home.
Virginia had no idea
her host was the general staff officer
of SOE's F Section—
the British spy agency's French networks.

After hearing Virginia's detailed description
of her ambulance exploits,
Bodington was intrigued.
And after learning
of Virginia's devotion to France
and her fluency in French and German,
he had a hunch that this confident American woman
had extraordinary potential as a spy.

Of course Bodington also knew that a tall,
elegant woman with a wooden leg
was not at all what Winston Churchill,
the British prime minister,
had in mind when he ordered
his new spy agency to *set Europe ablaze.*
Churchill expected the SOE
to do much more than gather enemy intelligence.
He directed them to recruit, organize, and train
the French Resistance—
groups of French locals
dedicated to fighting
the Nazi occupation in France.

Trained volunteers would be needed
to sabotage and disrupt the Germans
with brutal surprise tactics, raids, and ambushes—
a guerrilla style of combat that Churchill called
a most "ungentlemanly"
new form of undercover warfare.

Virginia didn't have a French passport
or a strong French accent,
but she exuded confidence, common sense,
and courage—qualities the SOE desperately needed.

On January 15, 1941,
The day after Bodington met Virginia
he wrote this memo:

Miss Virginia Hall who works at the American U.S. Embassy
. . . talked in my house last night
of wanting to go for about a month to France. . . .
It strikes me that this lady,
a native of Baltimore,
might well be used for a mission.

Once the extensive background checks
were complete and Virginia
was given official clearance,
Bodington invited her
to join the SOE's F Section.

After numerous rejections
for being disabled,
being American,
and being a woman,
Virginia had been offered
the chance to return to France
to fight for its freedom.

Prepared for a future
full of danger and hardship,
Virginia accepted Bodington's offer.

This wasn't the path
Virginia had dreamed of as a child—
but neither had she dreamed
of losing her father or her leg.

Adapting to new circumstances
and overcoming overwhelming obstacles—
these were proving to be
Virginia's hallmark qualities.

All her experiences and sacrifices
were finally coming together.
In the summer of 1941,
Virginia Hall and Cuthbert
would head back to France—

this time as a British spy.

GERMAINE

While Britain strengthened its army,
the SOE—also known as "Churchill's Secret Army"
and the "Baker Street Irregulars"—
was busy training spies.
Virginia, however, did not receive
the same extensive sabotage training
in *irregular warfare* tactics
that the other recruits received.

SOE was in urgent need
of her services as a liaison—
the point person for SOE agents—
and an intelligence agent—
someone to gather enemy secrets
and communicate them
back to Baker Street headquarters.

**1937. This photo of Virginia was most likely
taken in Italy, her first post after her amputation
recovery. Her mother accompanied Virginia to
Venice and stayed with her for six months.**

Virginia made the most of her brief training
before leaving for France.
She learned to conceal spy secrets
inside her belongings, her clothes,
and even inside Cuthbert's aluminum foot—
though she preferred keeping
intelligence in her head,
in case of capture.
Virginia learned to pick locks,
search desks, and tell lies—
all without being noticed.

Recognizing and evading
enemy spies on her trail
were skills she would need
to master to stay alive,
but it wouldn't be easy
for a tall American beauty
to blend in and disappear.
Fortunately, Virginia's experiences
on the stage and behind the curtain
in school theater productions came in handy.
She would need to alter her looks
by changing her mannerisms,
makeup, and hairstyles
as effortlessly as changing her clothes.

Virginia received instruction
in how to withstand interrogations and torture,
and, if necessary,
sacrifice her own life
to protect the identity of other agents.

Living in Nazi-controlled France,
working in consulates,
driving army ambulances—
all these experiences
gave Virginia a firm foundation
for her spy training.

But running wild at Boxhorn Farm
had certainly provided her
with invaluable physical training.
Even with Cuthbert, Virginia could canoe, ride a horse, and
shoot a gun.
She could swim, ski, ride a bicycle,
and climb a mountain
just as well as most men.

Virginia wasn't concerned
about physical hardships.
As an American woman,
she knew her biggest challenge
would be gaining the trust of French locals
and the respect of male British agents.

On April 1, 1941,
Virginia was given her SOE identity—
Germaine, Agent 3844—
making her SOE's first female F Section agent.
She was directed to set up a base in Vichy,
the capital of Pétain's puppet government.
It would be difficult to navigate
this small city crawling with Nazis
to gather German intelligence.

Virginia knew that once she arrived in Vichy,
she would be on her own
without protection or backup.
She understood that captured females
did not have the same
prisoner of war protections as males.

Even her SOE superiors in London
thought she only had
a fifty-fifty chance
of surviving this dangerous mission.

The thirty-five-year-old
American woman with a wooden leg
was determined to prove them wrong.

GERMAINE A.K.A. BRIGITTE

In August 1941
a red-haired Agent Germaine
entered France with a most convenient cover.
Her papers and passport
identified her as Virginia Hall,
a *stringer*—freelance journalist—
for the *New York Post*.

It was Virginia's clever idea
to use the cover
of an American journalist.
This would take care of any doubts
about her French accent
and would provide her a reason
to travel and ask questions.

George Backer,
the publisher of the *Post,*
was thrilled to have
an American correspondent inside France
to report on local war conditions.
He acted as if he wasn't aware
that Virginia's work as a reporter
was only a cover for spy activities.

Virginia quickly adjusted
to her new roles and slipped
in and out of her identities with ease.
As Virginia the reporter,
she detailed
for American readers
the hardships of French life
under growing Nazi pressure.
As Germaine the spy,
Virginia secretly gathered and relayed
German intelligence
for her Baker Street bosses.

But French locals
knew her as *Brigitte LeContre.*
With her natural charm
and obvious love for France,
Virginia earned the trust
of those who were suspicious of foreigners.

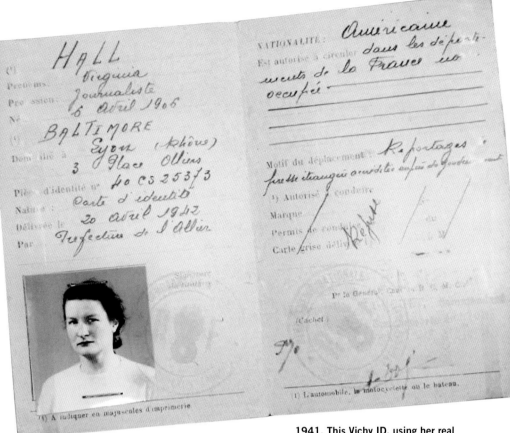

She even befriended policemen and officials who provided her with German intelligence and added security. A historian wrote, *She seems to have totally bewitched everybody who knew her.*

One of Virginia's most helpful contacts and trusted friends, Suzanne Bertillon, was the local foreign press censor who reviewed and approved Virginia's *New York Post* articles.

The SOE depended on Virginia's articles
to provide them with essential news
of food rations, curfews, and restrictions
that French locals suffered.

As a neutral American journalist,
Virginia could ask questions
and report valuable intelligence to London
by detailing the increasing hardships
imposed on the French by the Germans.

At times Virginia used sarcasm
to describe the appalling food shortages in France:

France would be a paradise
for vegetarians
if there were plenty of milk and cheese and butter,
but I haven't yet seen any butter
and there is little milk.

Virginia never hesitated
to paint a realistic portrait
of the toll the German restrictions
had taken on the French:

Many families are divided brutally . . .
And many sons, brothers, fathers and fiances
are still prisoners in Germany.
Naturally, people who are separated
from those they love,
whose relatives are still prisoners,
are living under constant mental strain,
which reacts upon their physical condition.

Suzanne, Virginia's *unofficial Vichy correspondent*,
provided much more than clearance
for Virginia's articles.
She connected Agent Germaine
with over ninety resistance informants
throughout France.
Virginia earned the trust
of farmers, laborers, businessmen, and politicians,
who risked their lives
to divulge top-secret intelligence
of German troop movements,
weapons production,
and military base locations.

Thanks to her new contacts,
Virginia was able to report the secret location
of a German submarine base in Marseilles, France,
which the British would later bomb.

Much to the surprise and delight
of the SOE back in London,
Virginia was proving to be
one of their most productive spies in France.
But it was becoming increasingly difficult
for her to safely function
from a base
where Pétain's government officials
and Vichy police
worked in sync with the Nazis.

After a month
of collecting intelligence
about the Vichy government
without being discovered,
Agent Germaine decided to move
to a safer location.

Virginia set up a new base in Lyon, France—
a larger city, tucked between two rivers
and close to neutral Switzerland's border.

Lyon's maze-like streets
and surrounding floodplains
offered better cover for SOE spies,
more fields for parachute supply drops,
and easier escape routes
for downed pilots and agents.
While Vichy was the
capital of Pétain's unoccupied zone,
Lyon was the center of the French Resistance.

Virginia was anxious
to set up a base there,
but finding a place to rent in town
was impossible.
Thousands of refugees
who had escaped Nazi persecution
in other countries had already flooded Lyon.
Unable to find a hotel room,
Virginia discovered a most unusual
safe haven among nuns
in the Sainte-Élisabeth convent,
just outside of town.

Now with dyed light brown hair
pulled back in a bun,
Virginia bicycled back and forth
between town and convent—
between reporter and spy.

The nuns at Sainte-Élisabeth
not only sympathized
with Virginia's mission,
they offered their convent
as a trusted safe house—
a hiding place
for her agents and escapees.

But Virginia needed
a more centrally located base
where she could meet her secret contacts.
So, as soon as a room was available,
Virginia used forged papers
to check into the Grand Hotel
with her French name, Brigitte LeContre.

Virginia's street-side room
gave her a view
of the comings and goings in town.
The hotel's many exits,
as well as its easy access
to the tram and the American consulate,
gave Virginia just the security and flexibility
she needed for a quick escape.

But living in a hotel
for long periods of time
was risky for a spy,
so Virginia set up a new base
in a nearby apartment
where she quickly proved to be
a most dependable liaison—
the point person for almost every agent
sneaking in or out of France.

She amazed fellow agents
by her efficient and compassionate assistance
in providing them with money, food,
shelter, papers, and maps.
A grateful British agent described
the impact Virginia had on SOE agents—
If you sit in [her] kitchen long enough
you will see most people pass through
with one sort of trouble or another
which [she] promptly deals with.

It wasn't long before Virginia
earned a new trusted contact—
George Whittinghill.
As the American vice consul of Lyon,
Whittinghill was free
from the routine searches of Nazi guards
that French travelers had to endure.

No one knew that Virginia's intelligence reports
were tucked into the diplomatic pouch
that Whittinghill carried
to the American embassy
in Bern, Switzerland.

And no one knew that
after Virginia's spy secrets
were transported from Bern
to the Baker Street headquarters in London,
SOE messages and money
made their way safely back to Virginia
hidden in Whittinghill's pouch.

MARIE

A master at juggling multiple identities
and responsibilities,
Virginia organized her own spy network
called Heckler.

Now known by her spy contacts as *Marie Monin*,
Virginia arranged SOE parachute drops
of food, weapons, and money
for British agents and French Resistance fighters.

She recruited local couriers
to deliver supplies and spy secrets.
She provided forged papers,
medical assistance, and safe houses
for agents and SOE pilots
who had been shot down
and escaped capture.

Virginia faced dangers
and obstacles every day
as Heckler's leader,
but her greatest challenge was getting
skilled wireless radio operators.

The radios, code-named *pianos*,
provided the only direct line of communication
between SOE headquarters in London
and field agents in France.

Without skilled *pianists*—
wireless operators—
news of German movements
couldn't be reported,
parachute drops of supplies
couldn't be arranged,
and plans for downed pilots and escapees
couldn't be made.

As a field agent,
Virginia didn't have her own radio.
Radio operators were specially trained
and had to stay constantly on the move
to avoid capture.

The radios were cleverly hidden
inside suitcases,
but when in use
their wireless signals
were easily traced
by radio detection devices
of the Gestapo,
the Nazi secret police.
Because pianists were often captured
with evidence in hand—
a suitcase radio—
they faced the almost certain fate
of torture, prison, and death.

Despite not having
a wireless operator
to report her intelligence
back to London,
Virginia had more than proven
her worthiness to the SOE.

One of her comrades reported that
practically every F Section agent
sent to France during this period
was in touch with her,
and she helped them in every possible way,
providing papers, cover, etc.
and looking after them when in difficulties.

Word traveled quickly
throughout the French underground
that Marie Monin—
also known as
la dame qui boite,
the lady who limps—
was now running
the largest F Section spy network
in the free zone of France.

The Gestapo and Vichy police
intensified their search
for the elusive leader and her network.
In October the luck of F Section spies turned sour
when the Vichy police
captured a British radio operator
just after his parachute
landed off course in Lyon.

In his pocket they found
a map of an SOE safe house
called Villa des Bois.
The Vichy police,
aligned with the Gestapo
and every bit as brutal,
cleverly sent SOE agents
a phony invitation
for a gathering at the villa
to take place on October 24, 1941.

Although Virginia enjoyed
the company of her fellow agents,
she was wary of group gatherings.
Trusting her own instincts,
she stayed home that night.

Unfortunately,
almost all the F Section agents
and the two radio operators in the free zone
walked right into the Vichy police trap
when they entered the Villa des Bois.
Every essential agent and radio operator
in the entire area
were captured in one night's bust.

All were jailed and tortured.
Fiercely loyal to her comrades,
Virginia was determined to find a way
to break them free.

The SOE was devastated
by the loss of these invaluable men.
The new F Section chief, Maurice Buckmaster,
now depended on Virginia
to hold the French spy networks together.
Without radio operators,
she was the only agent left in France
who could communicate with Baker Street—
thanks to Whittinghill's diplomatic pouch.

The successful Villa des Bois bust
made life in Lyon more dangerous
for anyone who even appeared sympathetic
to the French Resistance—
especially Virginia.

The Gestapo and Vichy police
weren't the only ones
searching for Heckler's leader.
The Milice—the French paramilitary—
and Abwehr—the German intelligence agency
similar to the SOE—
also had orders to hunt down
Marie of Lyon and all her contacts.

With traitors and trackers everywhere,
Virginia cautiously chose her confidants.
Two Lyon assistants proved to be
among her most trustworthy.

Dr. Jean Rousset,
code name *Pépin*,
earned Virginia's highest praise—
she called him
her *very most valuable assistant.*

The doctor used his office
as a letter box—
a post for dropping
and picking up spy messages—
to avoid personal contact.

Not only did Rousset secretly treat
injured and ill resistance fighters,
he even converted a floor
above his office
into a fake insane asylum—
the perfect safe house
for Heckler agents and downed pilots.

Madame Germaine Guérin,
a fearless local Frenchwoman,
also contributed greatly
to Heckler's successes.
She provided food, fuel,
clothing, and safe houses
for Virginia's escapees.

Rousset and Guérin
sent valuable contacts Virginia's way.
A new steady stream
of resistance fighters
in need of assistance
passed through Virginia's door
and Rousset's office.
Secret signals and pass phrases
were frequently changed
to avert the unwelcome threat
of a double agent—
a spy pretending to work for one side
while spying for the other.

Despite the discomforts, disappointments,
and dangers, Virginia never let down her guard.
She knew that a careless mistake
could end in disaster for herself
and her Heckler contacts.

1941. Japan's two-hour surprise attack on Pearl Harbor resulted in 2,403 deaths and the destruction of nineteen US Navy ships. The USS *West Virginia* and USS *Tennessee* in this photo on the left were destroyed. The USS *Arizona* on the right sunk.

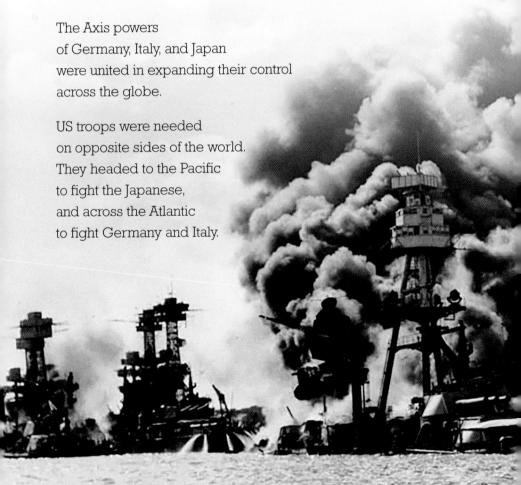

Virginia was shocked,
along with the rest of the world,
by the news on December 7, 1941,
that Japanese forces bombed Pearl Harbor—
the US naval base in Hawaii.

The following day,
The United States declared war on Japan
And entered World War II.

Three days later,
Japan's allies,
Germany and Italy,
declared war on the United States.

The Axis powers
of Germany, Italy, and Japan
were united in expanding their control
across the globe.

US troops were needed
on opposite sides of the world.
They headed to the Pacific
to fight the Japanese,
and across the Atlantic
to fight Germany and Italy.

Now that America
had joined the Allied fight
against the Germans,
Virginia could no longer
count on her cover
as an American journalist
to keep her safe in France—
she was considered the enemy.

Because of the extreme danger
and likelihood of being captured there,
SOE agents were generally ordered
to return to the safety of London
after three months in the field.
But when Baker Street
directed Virginia to return,
she insisted on staying.

Her job had been to assist
the safe passage of agents
and French sympathizers.
As long as F Section agents
were still in harm's way,
she wasn't about to leave them behind.

Bold but never careless,
Virginia agreed to move
to a new location.

In June 1942, after ten months in Lyon,
Virginia had proven to be an expert
at slipping in and out
of her various identities.
Depending on who she was meeting,
Virginia would change her name, her voice,
her hair, her makeup, and her clothes
as easily as she changed her location.
Her caution and cleverness
managed to keep Virginia
just out of the reach of Nazi spy hunters.

Virginia not only refused
to leave behind agents and downed pilots,
she was determined
to free *Clan Cameron*—
the code name for the group of SOE agents
and radio operators who had been arrested
at the Villa des Bois bust
and were now facing execution
in Mauzac prison.

Every Gestapo agent in Lyon
was looking for Agent Marie.
It was far too dangerous
for her to visit the prisoners,
even in disguise.
So Virginia was thrilled
when Gaby Bloch,
the wife of one of the prisoners,
volunteered to help her
break the Clan Cameron
out of jail.

Under Virginia's direction,
this fearless Jewish Frenchwoman
proved to be a better spy
than many trained SOE agents.

On her regular trips
to visit her husband, Jean Pierre-Bloch,
Gaby snuck escape tools
hidden inside laundry,
books, and food deliveries
past the prison guards.

If caught smuggling,
Gaby would most certainly
be tortured and jailed,
but she never hesitated
or showed fear when searched
on her way in and out of Mauzac.

Virginia coached Gaby
to recruit prison guards
to assist in the escape,
and she provided money
so Gaby could bribe them.
Virginia also arranged
the escapees' false ID papers,
train tickets, and safe houses
to aid their secure return to London.

To ensure a flawless escape,
the Clan Cameron prisoners
needed a wireless radio
to relay immediate messages.
Of course, Gaby could never
smuggle something as large
as a radio into the prison.
So Virginia devised a plan
that fooled the guards—
and even surprised the prisoners.

No one suspected
that the seventy-year-old priest
making pastoral visits
to the Clan Cameron
had snuck a wireless radio
into the prison barracks.
Confined to a wheelchair
after losing both legs
in World War I,
the priest breezed past security
hiding a wireless radio under his robe.

Soon the prisoners were
sending coded messages
directly to Baker Street in London
from their barracks.

Virginia's meticulous planning
and these invaluable deliveries
prepared Clan Cameron
for their escape.

It was up to the eleven prisoners—
and one helpful guard—
to make the break
without being caught.

In twelve well-planned minutes,
twelve well-trained escapees
snuck out of their barracks
in the middle of a dark July night
using a key that had been crafted
from the lid of a sardine can.

They hopped
from shadow to shadow
beneath the brightly lit watchtowers
to cross the prison yard.

And then, in total darkness,
they crawled through
a pre-cut section of
the barbed wire fencing—
their stomachs protected
by a piece of carpet.
Thanks to Virginia's arrangements,
Gaby's courageous contributions,
a flawless escape,
and a lot of luck,
every one of the Clan Cameron
made it safely back to London.

News of Virginia's jailbreak success
thrilled the SOE—
and enraged the Nazis.

Commanded by Hitler,
hundreds of new Gestapo agents
flooded the free zone with the urgent order
to capture and arrest the Heckler leader
code-named Marie.

Hitler's brutal Gestapo chief,
Klaus Barbie—known as the *Butcher of Lyon*
for his torture and killing
of thousands of captured Jews
and resistance fighters—
was obsessed with capturing
la dame qui boite, the lady who limps.
Barbie had no idea
of Marie's real identity
when one of his agents reported him saying
he would give anything to get his hands on that Canadian.

Barbie was also unaware that Abwehr agents
were very close to catching the "Limping Lady."

Just as Virginia had recruited nuns and a priest
to fight against the Nazis,
Abwehr sent its own "priest"
to break through Heckler's tight network.

From the first time
she met Abbé Robert Alesch
at Dr. Rousset's office
in the summer of 1942,
Virginia had an uneasy feeling about him—
particularly his German accent.
The *abbé*—French priest—
explained his accent
by claiming to be from the Alsace region
of France on the border of Germany.

He was known for his sermons
supporting the French Resistance—
but that was just a cover.
His faith was not with the church
or with the resistance.
The double agent
had more selfish plans.
Driven by greed,
Alesch aimed to get rich
by pretending to be a courier
for the resistance
while he sold their secrets to the Nazis.

Virginia mistrusted the pushy priest,
who had insisted on meeting her face to face
and had asked for the names of Heckler agents.
But Alesch impressed Rousset
with all the right passwords
and secret code names.

The abbé's deliveries of
German intelligence, maps, and photographs
persuaded Virginia
to push her suspicions aside
and give Alesch money and his own wireless radio.

Virginia should have trusted her gut.

**Maurice Buckmaster, leader of
Britain's SOE spy agency, relays
Virginia's distrust of Abbé Alesch,
a double agent for the Nazis.**

Copy in c.11. v.3 -   H4
                                                            Tp.

Information given on ABBÉ ALESCH by
Colonel M.J. Buckmaster.

Abbé ALESCH was working for an organisation in touch
with M.I.6. (Commander Dunderdale). This was a Polish
organisation and owing to many arrests the circuit was
closed down some time in 1942. We received a message from
"V.H.", saying that she had been approached by a member of
WOL,(this is said to stand for War Office Liaison). The
Abbe asked "V.H." to inform LONDON that whilst he had lost
contact with the group he had some interesting information
to transmit in the form of microphotos. He asked for funds.
After consultation with Mr. Green we agreed to send out two
sums of money via DF. "V.H." was not impressed by the Abbe
and thought him "phoney". We instructed her to cut all contact with him and informed Commander Dunderdale accordingly.
The Abbe's "phoneyness" was later confirmed by BERNE.

Further information on him may be found on "V.H.'s"
file in BERNE telegrams and filed correspondence with
Commander Dunderdale.

Because of Alesch's deceptions,
the Abwehr got just what they needed
from Heckler communications
to identify and capture SOE agents
in another French spy circuit in Paris.
With a radio and codes,
they secretly intercepted
Baker Street messages
and sent false information
back to SOE in London.
Virginia made the mistake
of meeting with Alesch twice,
giving him the opportunity
to make a description
of her appearance.

Suspicious of Alesch's loyalties,
Virginia never trusted him
enough to share her name or her address.
She radioed her concerns
about him to Baker Street,
and while she waited for their response,
she cut off all contact with him.

MARIE A.K.A. PHILOMENE

Fortunately for Virginia,
Abwehr hadn't yet
passed along the names
of her Heckler contacts
to the Gestapo.
They were waiting to
intercept more intelligence
before hunting down and arresting
the Heckler circuit.
Writing back to London as *Philomene* on September 9, 1942,
Virginia shared her concern
the enemy was closing in on her:
My address has been given to Vichy,
although not my name,
but it wouldn't be hard to guess . . .
I think my time is about up.

Virginia's SOE superiors
and her *New York Post* boss
pressured her again to return
to the safety of London.
But after thirteen months in France,
Virginia was still able to convince them
that she needed to stay,
despite the danger.

She was set on organizing
another prison break—
this time for two captured agents
code-named *Alex* and *Fabian*.

Knowing that Virginia
was every agent's best hope
for a safe journey in or out of France,
SOE officials gave in to Virginia's pleadings
to remain in Lyon—
and her promise to once again
move to a safer location in town.

In November 1942
Virginia abruptly changed her mind
about staying in Lyon
when she learned
of Operation Torch—
the US and British
invasion of French North Africa.

Threatened by this successful Allied attack,
Hitler decided to tighten his grip on Europe
and take complete control of France.
There was no longer a free zone,
and all the borders were closing.

To make matters even worse,
Klaus Barbie was doubling down
on his efforts to capture Marie Monin.
He was enraged that
the mysterious Heckler leader
was still on the loose.
He put the Limping Lady
at the top of the Gestapo's most wanted list.
A sketch of Virginia was posted
throughout the area with Barbie's directive—
The woman who limps is one of the most dangerous
    Allied agents in France.
We must find and destroy her.

ARAMIS
1944

HECKLER

This sketch of Virginia was drawn by Henri Laussucq, also known as Henri Lassot. This professional artist and elderly SOE and OSS agent accompanied her to France on her second mission. The Germans had no photographs of Virginia (Marie Monin), the mysterious female spy who the Gestapo and Abwehr nicknamed *Artemis*, a Canadian or English woman with a limp—*la dame qui boite*. Lorna Catling, Virginia's niece described Dindy as having a slight swing in her stride, not a limp.

Virginia, now using the code name *Philomene*,
hated to leave without alerting
her Heckler team,
but the risk was too great,
and there was too little time
to contact them.

The only question now was,
did Virginia have enough time
to make her own escape?

Virginia headed south for Perpignan—
a French town
near the Spanish border.

Border troops and mountain patrols
were flooding the area
in search of escapees
on their way to neutral Spain.

Avoiding capture
at train stations and checkpoints
kept Virginia on high alert,
but these initial obstacles
would prove to be the easiest part
of her journey to safety.
To reach Spain—and freedom—
the Limping Lady would have to cross
the snow-packed Pyrenees Mountains.

Traversing the perilous peaks in the summer
would challenge the most experienced hiker.
Virginia knew that a woman with a wooden leg
crossing them in November
had little chance of survival.

As the Nazis closed in on Perpignan,
Virginia put her faith, and her life,
in the hands of a *passeur*—
a French mountain guide.

She was lucky to find one
willing to lead a woman
up an eight-thousand-foot icy peak—
more than a mile and a half high.
There was no way
Virginia was going to
tell him about Cuthbert.

Virginia requested
an immediate departure,
but the passeur
wasn't ready to leave.
He was waiting
for three other escapees—
two Frenchmen and a Belgian captain—
to come up with the steep fare of twenty thousand francs
for their crossing.

With each passing hour,
Virginia's chances of escape grew slimmer
as Nazi troops swarmed the borders.

The escapees could not afford to pay,
and Virginia could not afford to wait.
She paid their passage
and the group disappeared
into the white.

Deep snow,
steep cliffs,
freezing temperatures,
and biting winds—
nothing, not even being hunted
by the Gestapo, the Abwehr, and the Milice,
could match the terror and the pain
Virginia experienced
crossing the Pyrenees.

Yet Virginia did not complain.
She knew passeurs
were often ruthless,
willing to leave the weak behind.
She would not ask for help
or stop to tend to
her blistered and bloody stump.

Once again
Virginia would need to depend
on her strength and her will
to survive the journey.

With echoes of
her father's dreamlike whisper
telling her to fight on,
Virginia dragged Cuthbert
across the snow-packed peaks.

Virginia kept up with the men—
and kept Cuthbert a secret.

Once they climbed six thousand feet
to Mantet Pass,
the passeur guided them
to the shelter of a shepherd's hut.
After Virginia managed to
privately tend to her raw stump
and change her bloody sock,
she sent a brief message
back to London on a wireless radio
found inside the hut.

She tapped out that she was safe, and added—

CUTHBERT IS BEING TIRESOME, BUT I CAN COPE

If Virginia hadn't been in so much pain,
she might have laughed
at the response
from the receiving agent in London,
who was neither aware of her disability
nor the name of her wooden leg—

IF CUTHBERT TIRESOME, HAVE HIM ELIMINATED

The remaining day and night
without rest or shelter
proved to be torturous.
The guide's warnings
of bear and wolf attacks
kept them alert
as they navigated their difficult decline.

It was nearly impossible
for Virginia to find firm footing
as she struggled to keep her balance
on a metal foot she could not feel.
Struggling to see and breathe
in the thin icy air,
Virginia wondered
for the first time in her life
if she had met a challenge
she could not survive.

At last, after three days
of torturous conditions,
the escapees finally reached
the Spanish border town
of San Juan de las Abadesas.

Nearly delirious
from the most terrifying experience of her life,
Virginia and her hiking companions
snuck to the train station
in the pre-dawn darkness.

With less than an hour to wait
for safe passage
to the American consulate in Barcelona,
the exhausted escapees were cornered
by the Spanish police.

The spy who eluded the Abwehr
and outsmarted the Gestapo
was arrested with her companions
for illegally crossing the border
as *undocumented and destitute refugees.*

For the first time in her life,
Virginia was stuck behind bars.

Separated from
her three companions,
who had been sent
to a Spanish prison camp,
Virginia spent her days
plotting her own jailbreak
while forming a close bond
with one of her cellmates.

Virginia had no doubt
that the American consulate in Barcelona
would arrange for her release,
but her jailers ignored
her pleas to contact them.

Fortunately, Virginia's cellmate
was happy to offer her assistance.
Immediately after her release,
she delivered a message
from Virginia to the consulate.

After six weeks in prison,
Virginia was finally free.

A lot had happened
since Virginia narrowly escaped
her post in Lyon.

She had no way of knowing
that she had been right all along
about Abbé Alesch—
he was not what he had preached.

Alesch had made a fortune
as a double agent.
The SOE paid him
to be a resistance courier
while the Germans paid him
for the names and locations
of Virginia's Heckler agents.

The uncertain fate of her comrades
haunted Virginia.
She needed to return to France
as soon as possible
to find them and rejoin the fight.

While she had been away,
the resistance circuits
she had helped build
inside the free zone
had grown and strengthened.
Using guerrilla warfare tactics,
French fighters were successfully sabotaging German troops
by attacking trains, roads, planes, and factories.
Virginia couldn't stand being removed
from the missions she had helped organize.

No one had greater respect
for Virginia's accomplishments
than the SOE F Section chief, Maurice Buckmaster.
And no one had a better understanding
of Klaus Barbie's obsession with capturing her.

Buckmaster firmly refused Virginia's request
to return to France—

You are really too well-known in the country
and it would be wishful thinking believing that you could
escape detection
for more than a few days . . .
We do not want to give him [Barbie] even half a chance
by sending in anyone as remarkable as yourself.

Disappointed, Virginia reluctantly headed
to a new post in Madrid, Spain, in May 1943.

Arrangements were again made
for her to use the cover
of an American journalist—
this time for the *Chicago Times*.
Her instructions were to set up
escape routes and safe houses
for resistance fighters passing through Spain.

While Spain's dictator, Francisco Franco,
was aligned with the Axis powers,
he kept peace with his European neighbors
by remaining neutral in the war.
Spain was filled with German spies,
and Virginia still needed
to guard her identity
while she assisted
resistance efforts there.
But after leading
one of the most successful spy networks
in Nazi-occupied France,
Virginia felt useless in Madrid,
so far from the action.
She requested a transfer
after only four months
and didn't hesitate
to express her disappointment
to Buckmaster—

When I came out here
I thought that I would be able
to help F section people,
but I don't and can't.
I am not doing a job.
I am simply
living pleasantly and wasting time.
It isn't worthwhile, and after all,
my neck is my own, and if I am willing to get a crick in it
because there is a war on,
I do think . . . . well, anyhow,
I put it up to you.

When Virginia returned to London
she tried, once again,
to persuade Buckmaster
to send her back to France.

She knew the resistance
had grown quite a bit
after Germany passed a law
that sent Frenchmen between the ages
of twenty and thirty-four
to Nazi labor camps.
To avoid capture, many of these men
fled to the mountains and hid out in forests
where they formed small bands
of local French Resistance fighters
called Maquis.

Virginia knew that the untrained warriors
needed instruction in guerrilla warfare.
These more *ungentlemanly*
warfare tactics were needed
to sabotage the Nazis
while the Allied armies
prepared for D-Day—
a massive surprise Allied invasion
that would provide the military might
France would need to stop the Nazis.
Virginia also knew the Maquis
needed trained radio operators
to keep communications open
with the SOE which would support them.

So in January 1944,
Virginia began her wireless radio training.
She had hoped that
once she was a qualified radio operator
Buckmaster would change his mind.
Unfortunately he remained steadfast,
reminding her that she was still at the top
of Barbie's most wanted list.
He would not send her back.

Used to navigating dead ends,
Virginia decided it was time to make a change.

Just as Virginia was looking for a way
to return to France to support the resistance,
America's new spy agency—
the Office of Strategic Services—
was looking for experienced agents and radio operators
to help Maquis fighters prepare for D-Day.
These local resistance groups
were proving to be most helpful
in gathering German intelligence
and sabotaging German troops.

When Virginia learned
that the risk-taking OSS director, Wild Bill Donovan,
was willing to send her back
into Nazi-occupied France
as a radio operator,
she decided she wanted to transfer.

Proud to represent her own country,
Virginia was disappointed
that she could not convince the OSS
to send her back without a male commander.
Female agents—
even the legendary Heckler leader—
could not lead a mission.

So, on a moonless March night in 1944,
Virginia crossed the English Channel to France
in a torpedo boat with Henri Lassot,
a much older and less experienced agent,
code-named *Aramis*.

This time Virginia would sneak
back into France
as *Agent Diane*,
carrying her own suitcase radio
and wearing a disguise
that would fool even her mother.

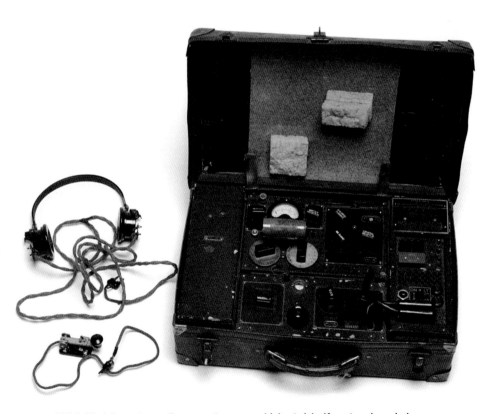

1944. Virginia sent countless secret messages back to London on this Type 3, Mark II suitcase radio on her second trip to occupied France. The new US spy agency, the OSS, was in desperate need of wireless radio operators who bravely shouldered the important responsibility of transmitting communications. They also carried the highest risk. If captured, a wireless operator would most likely be tortured and killed. When the SOE refused to send her back to occupied France, Virginia got her wireless radio training and switched to the OSS. Virginia's suitcase radio is on permanent display at the International Spy Museum in Washington, DC.

DIANE A.K.A. MARCELLE MONTAGNE

With dyed gray hair,
bulky peasant clothes,
and a shuffle to disguise her limp,
secret agent Diane
arrived safely in Paris
with Aramis by her side.
Meticulous about her disguise
in case of capture,
Virginia even had a dentist
give her French fillings
to avoid recognition
as an American.

While Virginia pretended
to be old and slow,
her partner proved to be slower.

This is Virginia's forged French birth certificate used in her second mission to France as an OSS agent.

After twisting his knee
upon their arrival,
Aramis struggled to walk
and carry bags.
She understood
that traveling together
as an old peasant couple
meant they were less likely
to be stopped by Nazi soldiers
at train stations and checkpoints.
But Aramis's complaints,
poor judgment, and big mouth
made her uneasy.
She needed to get away
from her careless partner
and out of Gestapo-infested Paris.

Virginia felt much safer
once she established her base
in a tiny village in La Creuse,
and Aramis returned to his base in Paris.
In a tiny shack without water or electricity,
Virginia began her new mission
with the cover of an old French milkmaid
named *Marcelle Montagne*.

Growing up with farm animals
on Boxhorn Farm
proved to be helpful training
for her spy work in rural France.
Thanks to Virginia's expert disguise,
skilled acting, and sharp instincts,
no one suspected that the milkmaid
who cooked meals and tended cows
for a local dairy farmer and his family
was *Artemis*—
the Nazi's code name for Virginia—
their most wanted spy.

And no one noticed
that when she took
the farmer's cows to pasture,
Virginia was scouting
remote fields for parachute drops
of weapons and supplies.

While she sold milk and cheese in the village,
Virginia not only secretly recruited
villagers and farmers to join the resistance,
she also eavesdropped on Nazi officers.
Fearless and fluent in German,
Virginia understood their every word—
and radioed the overheard Nazi military plans
back to OSS headquarters
from the farmer's attic.

Every radio operator's greatest fear
was a surprise raid by the Nazis.
One day while Virginia
was tapping out intelligence
in the farmer's attic,
she was startled by the sound
of a truck pulling up outside.

Virginia quickly hid her radio
and hurried downstairs.
She stayed cool
as German soldiers
were ordered to search inside.
She plotted possible escapes
as she heard the loud crashes
of overturned furniture.
Surely they had discovered her radio.
But when the soldiers came outside,
they weren't carrying her suitcase radio—
only cheese!

One of the soldiers
recognized her as the village cheesemaker.
He gave his thanks for the cheese,
threw coins at her feet, and drove away—
leaving behind a very relieved Virginia.

Virginia had narrowly escaped capture,
but some of her neighbors weren't so lucky.
A few days after the farmhouse raid,
she was horrified to see
the grotesque bodies of murdered villagers
left in the street by Nazis—
a stark warning for resistance sympathizers.

Virginia had too many unanswered questions.
What did the Nazis know?
Did they detect the radio signals
coming from the farmer's attic?
Were they suspicious of her visits from Aramis?

Deciding it was only a matter of time
before her peasant charade
and her unusual accent
would be discovered,
Virginia sent the OSS
an urgent wireless warning—

WOLVES ARE AT THE DOOR. STOP.

WILL BE IN CONTACT SOON. STOP.

Then she packed up her radio suitcase and disappeared.

In the late spring of 1944,
Virginia began moving
throughout central France,
still in peasant clothing,
to help organize
Maquis' sabotage missions
to delay and derail the Germans.
Virginia helped train fighters
and arrange supply drops
when she wasn't herding goats.

For three years
Virginia had sacrificed
and fought for the day
Allied armies would
return to France
to take back the country.
Finally on June 6, 1944,
that day had come.
The D-Day invasion
poured nearly 160,000 Allied troops
onto five beaches
in Normandy, France.
After the largest seaborne invasion
in history,
thousands of French locals
rushed to join Maquis groups
to fight the ruthless Germans
who were wreaking a path of destruction
on their way home.

1944. On June 6, 1944, the long-awaited D-Day arrived. This operation, code named *Overlord*, spilled nearly 160,000 Allied troops onto the beaches of Normandy, France, to unleash the largest amphibious invasion in history. Virginia was focused on assisting the French Resistance in sabotaging the Germans to enable the Allies to advance more quickly.

Now more than ever,
Maquis were needed
to cut off German transports
and communications.
Virginia helped train
the French freedom fighters
to poke holes in gas tanks
of Nazi cars and trucks.
They knocked down telephone wires,
blocked railroad tracks,
and blew up bridges.
They changed road signs
to set the Germans
in the wrong direction,
and they hid explosives
in piles of horse dung on the roads.

After organizing and training
hundreds of volunteers,
Virginia had proven she was
a remarkably successful guerrilla leader.
So it pained her
to not be given command
of a Maquis group of her own.
And because she was still at the top
of the Gestapo's most wanted list,
she was not allowed to join her men
on the secret sabotage missions
she helped plan.

It was essential for Virginia
to keep moving to avoid capture.
She received new orders
and headed south
in the Haute-Loire region.
A plateau in the hills
of Le Chambon-sur-Lignon
would provide the perfect landing fields
for the weapons and supply parachute drops
the local Maquis desperately needed.

LA MADONE

V irginia discovered
that the Chambon Maquis
offered their own set of obstacles.

Though united in their fight against the Germans,
the Maquis leaders
often disagreed on how to organize,
and many were bewildered
by the arrival of Agent Diane—
an American woman
with a terrible French accent,
who clearly had more experience
than all of them.

The Maquis leader, Pierre Fayol,
made it clear that while he expected Virginia
to arrange parachute deliveries
and provide money and supplies,
he would not be following her orders.

Virginia was used to proving
she was as capable as a man.
Now dressed in khakis and an army jacket,
she made it clear
that she expected the Maquis
to take her instruction
if they expected her
to arrange supply deliveries.

Fayol may have resented her leadership,
but Virginia built trusting relationships
with many of the other freedom fighters.
She bought bicycles
for herself and a small crew of loyal fighters
to aid in finding parachute drop locations.
Securing and relaying messages about safe sites
for parachute drops in the mountain region
was one of the most difficult
and important parts of her mission.

In four weeks' time
she would send thirty-seven
messages to London without being traced.
A devoted admirer even found a way
to use a bicycle and a car battery
to power Virginia's radio.
One of her bicycle messages
signaled a parachute delivery—
Les marguerites fleuriront ce soir
—the daisies will bloom tonight.

This Jeffrey Bass painting, *Les Marguerites Fleuriront ce Soir* ("the daisies will bloom tonight"), named for one of the codes that signaled an Allied airdrop, shows Virginia transmitting a wireless message back to London in 1944 from Leá Lebrat's farmhouse above the village of Le Chambon-sur-Lignon in the Haute-Loire. Leá's relative and Virginia's resistance comrade, Edmond Lebrat, pedals an adapted bicycle beside her, providing power from a car battery for Virginia's radio. In 2006, this painting was unveiled at a special ceremony at the French Ambassador's residence in Washington, DC, and is now in the CIA Fine Arts Collection.

Virginia more than lived up
to the promises she made
to the Chambon Maquis.

Night after moon-filled night,
metal cannisters dropped from the sky,
filled with not only the weapons and ammunition
needed to perform their missions—
but also money, clothes, boots,
and sweet treats like cookies and chocolate.

Virginia even received
her own personal cannisters
filled with her favorite tea,
letters from her mother,
and much-needed socks for Cuthbert.

Like clockwork, Virginia's men
raced to carry out her carefully planned
air drop recovery routine
to secure the secret shipments
in under fifteen minutes.
Teams split up to simultaneously
stamp out the small fires
that lit the makeshift runway,
cut the ropes from the metal cannisters,
fold the parachutes into bags,
load the heavy, metal cannisters
into ox-drawn carts,
and, without a thread of evidence left behind,
transport them to safe houses.

Amazed by her miraculous deliveries
of twenty-two parachute drops in all,
these Maquis fighters
would forever call Virginia
La Madone—
the Madonna of the Mountains.

Word spread about the successes
organized and led
by this mysterious woman.
Soon a small band of thirty fighters
grew to five companies
of over four hundred trained
Maquis soldiers.

Fayol and some of the other leaders
were happy to accept
the money and weapon deliveries,
but they still would only take orders
from their French superiors.

Virginia stayed focused on her mission.
She reported to the OSS—
as long as Gévolde and Fayol
were willing to do
sabotage and guerrilla work
I did not care about the fact
that they would not cooperate with me.

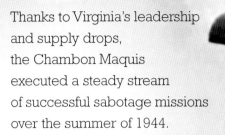

Thanks to Virginia's leadership
and supply drops,
the Chambon Maquis
executed a steady stream
of successful sabotage missions
over the summer of 1944.

In August, Virginia
directed guerrilla fighters
in the successful ambushes
of Nazi convoys
with courage and grit.
After a bold five-day attack
on a German convoy,
and without the aid
of official Allied troops,
Virginia and the Chambon Maquis
defeated the Nazis
in the area,
freeing the people
in the Haute-Loire region.

1944. B-17 Flying Fortresses
drop supplies to the Maquis
fighters in the Vercors region,
only a few hours away from
Virginia's location on the
Haute-Loire plateau.

Stories of La Madone's heroics
became legendary.
Even Pierre Fayol,
once Virginia's greatest critic,
became her most devoted fan.
After the war
his appreciation for her grew—

We know perfectly well
just how much we owe her.
Virginia's spirit soared above the plateau,
and for those who knew her from those days
she was forever "La Madone."

DIANE'S IRREGULARS

On August 25, 1944,
soon after Virginia helped free
the Haute-Loire from Nazi control,
the Germans surrendered Paris
to Allied troops.

While Paris may have been liberated,
Virginia knew the war
was far from over
where she was in central France.
Maquis missions were still needed
to combat the defeated and enraged Germans
as they continued their paths of destruction
across the French countryside.

Virginia was determined
to continue organizing
French Resistance missions
as Agent Diane,
but she needed more backup
from the OSS.

Thankfully, they agreed.
Finally, after years of organizing missions
without full authority,
Virginia had gotten what she wanted
from her superiors—
permission to recruit and command
her own Maquis.

1944. Virginia was excited to finally have command of her own Maquis unit of nineteen volunteers and permission to join the fight. Her loyal new backup agents, Lieutenant Henry Riley (on ground holding pup) and her future husband, Lieutenant Paul Goillot (on far right), helped train the young, rough local fighters in guerrilla warfare tactics to sabotage, harass, and ambush the retreating Germans. Her loyal group of scrappy fighters became known as the Diane Irregulars as a tribute to their leader, known only by her code name, *Diane*.

In early September,
Virginia prepared
for the midnight parachute drop
of two French American agents
sent to help her new mission.
She waited all night
for a plane that never arrived.

After landing way off target
in treetops over twenty miles away,
Paul Goillot and Henry Riley
untangled their parachutes,
gathered their supplies,
and made their way to Agent Diane.

While Paul and Henry
were at first hesitant
to follow the orders of a woman,
it didn't take long for them to see
that Virginia was a remarkably skilled
and courageous commander.

Under Virginia's direction,
Paul and Henry helped recruit and train
a new group of Maquis fighters
to continue sabotage missions
against the retreating Germans.

Virginia's new guerrilla recruits
called themselves the *Diane Irregulars*,
proving their devotion
to their courageous leader.

After years of planning missions
without being able to participate,
Virginia couldn't wait to join the fight
with her well-trained team.

But she would never have the chance.

The Allied armies had taken hold of France
more quickly than planned.
New orders were given—
the services of French Maquis
were no longer needed.

There would be no missions for Virginia
and her Diane Irregulars.

It was time for Virginia
to say farewell
to her loyal comrades—
all except Paul.
Virginia had formed
many friendships during the war,
but she had never
let herself fall in love.
The constant threat
of danger and death
kept Virginia's focus
on her missions and her own safety.
But Paul was different from anyone
she had ever met.
Aside from being a loyal combat partner,
Paul's humor and charm provided Virginia
much needed comfort and distraction
from the horrors of war.
Virginia didn't mind
that Paul was six inches shorter
and eight years younger—
he could cook meals, make repairs,
and solve problems with a wink and a smile.

Paul had not only earned Virginia's trust—
he had won her heart.

1944. Virginia is surrounded by her parachute reception
committee. Her command of the Diane Irregulars was
short-lived as the war in Europe ended shortly after their
training began. After spending much of her OSS service
disguised as an old French peasant, Virginia traded in her
long skirts for combat wear in the Haute-Loire.

DIANA

While the Germans had lost
their hold on France,
they were still hanging on
in neighboring countries.

Revered as the most
capable of all American agents,
Virginia was handpicked by
Director Donovan
to command an important
OSS secret mission in Austria
in the fall of 1944.

With the assurance
that Paul would be on her team,
Virginia, code-named *Diana*,
prepared for another dangerous mission
in the mountains.
But, after many months of frustrating delays,
their secret operation was brought
to a sudden halt before it even began.

1944. Thousands of French citizens line the Champs-Élysées on August 26 to celebrate the liberation of Paris from the Germans. Here they cheer Allied tanks and the French Second Armored Division as they pass through the Arc de Triomphe.

While British and American troops
took control of France,
their Soviet allies captured Berlin,
the capital of Germany.

Unwilling to face defeat,
Hitler killed himself on April 30, 1945.

One week later, on May 8,
the German Army surrendered.

World War II in Europe was finally over.

VIRGINIA

Virginia and Paul celebrated
the end of the war in Paris—
Paul's birthplace and Virginia's favorite city.

But it was far from the end
of Virginia's secret service.

While she focused
on getting back to the business
of defending freedom,
Virginia was surprised by the news
that President Harry S. Truman
wished to honor her
with the Distinguished Service Cross for
*extraordinary heroism in connection
with military operations against
an armed enemy.*

Virginia was not a fan of awards or praise.
As she told a friend in France—
*I don't want people to hear about what I did.
All I did was for love of France,
my second homeland.*

134

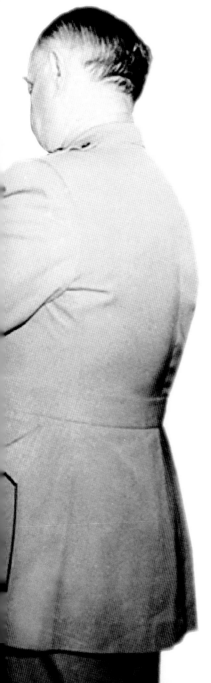

Besides, Virginia made it clear
that the less said
about her heroics the better,
when she explained—
> *Too many of my friends were killed
> because they talked too much.*

Wanting to protect her future as a spy,
Virginia declined a public ceremony
with President Truman.
Virginia—the only civilian woman
    in World War II
to have received this prestigious award—
agreed to accept her award
from her devoted director,
    Wild Bill Donovan,
in a private presentation.

1945. William Donovan, the director of the OSS, awards Virginia the Distinguished Service Cross (DSC) *for extraordinary heroism in connection with military operations against the enemy.* The only civilian female to receive the DSC for service during WWII, Virginia declined President Truman's invitation to award her publicly. Instead, to preserve her secret identity as a spy, she received her award privately with only her mother in attendance.

This is an undated photo of Virginia looking into a mirror. Throughout the war, Virginia remains true to herself and her convictions despite her ever-changing identities.

DINDY

Dindy, the once cantankerous
and capricious schoolgirl,
had certainly lived
a *most original* life.

And, as in most things
Dindy set out to do,
she had exceeded expectations,
even her own,
when she proclaimed
as a high school senior—

I must have liberty, withal as large a charter as I please.

Just as clever at skirting praise
as avoiding capture,
the adult Dindy—
the mysterious Virginia Hall—
shrugged off her extraordinary heroics
in helping to liberate France
with her characteristic humility—

Not bad for a girl from Baltimore

AFTERWORD: VIRGINIA HALL GOILLOT

Once the war was over, Virginia focused her energies on returning to Lyon to track down her loyal Heckler team. Virginia was devastated to learn that Abbé Alesch was responsible for the arrests of most all her Heckler comrades. Distraught that some of her brave volunteers had not survived, Virginia was relieved to find and reunite with Germaine Guérin and Dr. Jean Rousset. Sadly, she found her dear *Pépin* to be almost unrecognizable. After surviving eighteen grueling months at the Buchenwald concentration camp by serving as a prison doctor, Rousset's body and spirits were ravaged.

While Germaine was one of the few to live through the tortures of the Ravensbrück concentration camp, she was not only shattered from the horrors she had witnessed and endured, but she was also left penniless. Thanks to Virginia's persistent appeals to the British government, Germaine was granted compensation for her patriotic sacrifices.

Virginia tracked down and advocated for the compensation and recognition of many other surviving freedom fighters as well, but her most relentless pursuit was of the phony priest, Alesch. With the help of detailed accounts that she, Rousset, and Guérin offered French authorities, Alesch was finally arrested

138

and put on trial in Paris on May 25, 1948. This time no one was fooled by his lies. After a three-day trial for conspiring with the enemy, Alesch was found guilty and sentenced to death. On February 25, 1949, he was executed by firing squad.

After the war, Virginia continued her espionage work with the Central Intelligence Group, and when it was renamed the Central Intelligence Agency in 1947, she was their first female paramilitary officer and would become the CIA's first tenured female. After years of devoted service, Virginia remained loyal to the CIA until her mandatory retirement at age sixty.

Spy partners in war, Virginia and Paul remained devoted partners for life. Paul followed his dream of owning his own restaurant in Washington, DC, before devoting himself to caring for Virginia and their farm in Barnesville, Maryland. For the rest of her life, Virginia quietly suffered from relentless pain and discomfort due to Cuthbert, but that didn't keep her from enjoying retirement with Paul. Virginia found well-earned peace in gardening, making cheese, weaving, tending to her goats, entertaining guests, and spoiling her pack of adoring standard French poodles. The stoic spy was even known to feed them with a silver spoon.

Never one to talk about her heroic adventures, the mysterious Virginia Hall—*the limping lady, Marie of Lyon, the Madonna of the Mountains*—kept her spy secrets and her accolades to herself.

AUTHOR'S NOTE: AUNT DINDY

Having researched and written books about heroic spies and hometown heroes, I was intrigued to learn about Virginia Hall, the legendary World War II spy and Baltimore native. What I didn't expect to learn was that the woman known as the *Limping Lady*, the Gestapo's most wanted spy, had attended Roland Park Country School for twelve years—the same school my daughter attended nearly ninety years later. I was equally excited to learn that Virginia Hall, who passed away in 1982, still had family in Baltimore. It is a rare privilege to meet the relatives of my historical subjects, so I was thrilled to connect with Lorna Catling, Dindy's niece. What a surprise to discover that we live in the same neighborhood. I often describe my job of researching and sharing real-life stories as treasure hunting. I really struck gold finding Lorna, a real-life treasure, who so graciously and generously shared with me her memories and photographs of her extraordinary Aunt Dindy.

1945. Shortly after her return to Boxhorn Farm after World War II, Virginia enjoys the company of lambs, a turkey, and a French poodle in the barn. Later that year, she returned to Europe to continue her work in intelligence before joining the newly formed Central Intelligence Group in 1946, which would become the CIA a year later.

THE WHITE HOUSE

WASHINGTON

CITATION FOR DISTINGUISHED SERVICE CROSS

     Miss Virginia Hall, an American civilian in the employ of the Special Operations Branch, Office of Strategic Services, voluntarily entered and served in enemy occupied France from March to September 1944. Despite the fact that she was well known to the Gestapo because of previous activities, she established and maintained radio communication with London Head-quarters, supplying valuable operational and intelligence information, and with the help of a Jedburgh team, she organized, armed and trained three battalions of French Resistance Forces in the Department of the Haute Loire. Working in a region infested with enemy troops and constantly hunted by the Gestapo, with utter disregard for her safety and continually at the risk of capture, torture and death, she directed the Resistance Forces with extraordinary success in acts of sabotage and guerrilla warfare against enemy troops, installations and communications. Miss Hall displayed rare courage, perseverance and ingenuity; her efforts contributed materially to the successful operations of the Resistance Forces in support of the Allied Expeditionary Forces in the liberation of France.

                           /s/ Harry S. Truman

A true copy:

Frank L. Ball, Jr.
Major, AUS

Left: President Truman's 1945 citation for Virginia's DSC medal.

VIRGINIA HALL'S AWARDS AND HONORS

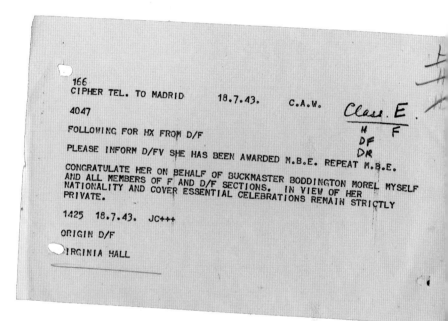

166
CIPHER TEL. TO MADRID   18.7.43.   C.A.W.   Class E.
4047   H   F
FOLLOWING FOR HX FROM D/F   DF
PLEASE INFORM D/FV SHE HAS BEEN AWARDED M.B.E. REPEAT M.B.E.   DR
CONGRATULATE HER ON BEHALF OF BUCKMASTER BODDINGTON MOREL MYSELF
AND ALL MEMBERS OF F AND D/F SECTIONS. IN VIEW OF HER
NATIONALITY AND COVER ESSENTIAL CELEBRATIONS REMAIN STRICTLY
PRIVATE.

1425 18.7.43. JC+++

ORIGIN D/F

VIRGINIA HALL

Congratulatory telegram for Virginia from SOE superiors on receiving
MBE—"Member of the Most Excellent Order of the British Empire"—for
her courageous work as a spy and liaison for the Resistance in France in
1941–1942. She kept her award secret so she could continue her work as an
undercover agent.

1943: King George VI honors Virginia as an honorary Member
of the Most Excellent Order of the British Empire.

1945: President Harry Truman wants to present the Distinguished
Service Cross to Hall in a special ceremony, but Hall declines a
public presentation to protect her anonymity as an active agent.

September 1945: In a private ceremony, Virginia's former OSS boss, General Donovan, presents the Distinguished Service Cross to Virginia—the only civilian woman to receive this honor in World War II—with only her mother in attendance.

March 16, 1946: France privately awards Virginia the high honor of the Croix de Guerre with palm for heroism in combat. Hall requested that the recognition be kept secret so she could continue her intelligence work. She keeps this illustrious honor a secret for the rest of her life. A 1973 fire in the French archives destroyed documentation of the award, but another source was recently uncovered.

1988: Virginia Hall is inducted into the inaugural class of the Military Intelligence Hall of Fame.

December 2006: French and British ambassadors honor her heroics at the French ambassador's home in Washington, DC, on the hundredth anniversary of her birth. Her niece, Lorna Catling, was presented with her aunt's award and accolades as a "true hero of the French Resistance."

2016: The Virginia Hall Expeditionary Center opens as a CIA field agent training facility at CIA headquarters. Virginia Hall is featured at a CIA museum exhibit representing Service, one of six pillars of the organization. She is the only woman to be recognized.

2019: Virginia Hall is inducted into the Maryland Women's Hall of Fame.

1928. Virginia's passport

Virginia Hall

the picture of the person to
whom this passport is issued

ACKNOWLEDGMENTS

I am forever grateful to Lorna Catling and her son, Brad, for their invaluable contributions and insights about their Aunt Dindy. They so generously shared family stories, memories, and photographs that brought Dindy to life for me, and hopefully for my readers. I would like to thank Sara Lichterman, Randy Burkett, and Janelle Neises at the CIA; Missie Mack and Abbey Pulcinella at Roland Park Country School; Debra Elfenbein, the special collections librarian at the Enock Pratt Free Library; and Christian Belena at the Franklin D. Roosevelt Library and Museum. I am grateful for the contributions of the renowned portraitist, Jeffrey Bass, and the acclaimed documentary filmmaker, Pierre Sauvage.

Special thanks to my brother, Charley, who sparked my interest in Virginia Hall years ago when he forwarded an article about the Baltimore spy who attended my daughter's school. I would also like to thank my first-round readers, Marcia Benshoof and my mother Coleen Davis, for their careful reviews and thoughtful insights. Thanks to my husband, Winn, for his limitless patience and encouragement and to Ann Matzke and my Camp Carolyn writing comrades for their support and companionship on this long and often lonely road. I am so grateful for the care and guidance I receive from my agent, Rachel Orr, who is the most enthusiastic and supportive advocate any writer could hope for. And finally, eternal thanks to the whole team at Calkins Creek, most especially my amazing editor, Carolyn Yoder, and associate editor Thalia Leaf.

Undated photo. Virginia learned to ride horses
as a child, and as an adult she rode every
chance she got in the US and overseas.

SOURCE NOTES

The source of each quotation in this book is found below. The citation indicates the first words of the quotation and its document source. The document sources are listed in the bibliography.

DINDY (page 10)

"Fighting Blade": Mugele, p. 4.

"She is, by her own confession, . . .": *Quid Nunc*, p. 12.

"I must have liberty, . . .": Ibid. Quote based on Shakespeare's play *As You Like It,* Act II, Scene 7, Lines 48–49.

"most original": *Quid Nunc,* p.12.

VIRGINIA (page 19)

"a lot of uninteresting required courses": VH letter to Rossiter, Feb 2, 1978, *Women in the Resistance* Papers, Box 3, University of Michigan Special Collection, quoted in Mitchell, p. 7.

VIRGINIA and CUTHBERT (page 32)

"amputation of a portion of a limb . . .": Letter from Sumner Welles to Francis R. Stewart, Sept 29, 1936, Virginia Hall State Department File, State Department General Records, RG 59/Box 526/Folder 123, NARA, quoted in Haines, p. 250.

"Why, Oh, Why do the regulations . . .": Memo for Secretary of State, FDR Presidential Library, Hyde Park, New York. Feb. 9, 1938.

"well taken care of" and "plenty of good food": *Baltimore Sun,*
June 12, 1940.

"well intentioned, but they . . .": Ibid.

"at the time of defeat . . .": From C.R.I., Feb. 2, 1943, Virginia Hall SOE
Personnel File, HS 9/647/4, British National Archives, quoted in
Mitchell, p. 23.

"set Europe ablaze": Winston Churchill quoted in *The Second World War
Diary of Hugh Dalton 1940–1945*, entry Monday, 22 July 1940. London:
Jonathan Cape, p. 62.

"a most 'ungentlemanly' new form of undercover warfare": Purnell,
"Virginia Hall," and Dalton, p.1.

"Miss Virginia Hall . . .": memo from Bodington to Marriott, SOE HS 9-674-4,
Virginia Hall Personnel File, Jan. 15, 1941, quoted in Demetrios, p. 77.

GERMAINE (page 61)

"irregular warfare . . .": British SOE, *How to become a Spy: The World War
II SOE Training Manual.* New York: Skyhorse Publishing, 2015, p. 4-5.

Carlomagno, "Women in a Man's War," p. 54.

GERMAINE A.K.A BRIGITTE (page 65)

"She seems to have totally . . .": Grose, p. 63.

"France would be a paradise . . .": Hall, "Vichy Exclusive."

"Many families are divided brutally . . .": Hall, "France's Rabbits on Strike."

"If you sit in [her] kitchen long enough . . .": Ben Cowburn's Personnel
File, SOE HS6-568, quoted in Purnell, *A Woman of No Importance*, p. 93.

MARIE (page 74)

"Practically every F Section agent . . .": commendation, Virginia Hall Personnel File HS 9/647/4703284, Nov. 21, 1944, British Archives.

"very most valuable assistant": Report sent to SOE by 'Marie,' Sept. 6, 1942, Hall SOE Personnel File, HS 9/674/4.

"He would give anything . . ." quoted in Ian Dear, *Sabotage and Subversion: The SOE and OSS at War.* Cheltenham, UK: The History Press, 2010, p. 164. Henry Newton Personnel File HS 9/1091/1, quoted in Vigurs, p. 42.

MARIE A.K.A. PHILOMENE (page 91)

"My address has been given . . .": Message from Philomene, Virginia Hall Personnel File HS 9/647/4703284, Sept. 21, 1942, British Archives.

"The woman who limps is . . .": Fayol, *Le Chambon-sur-Lignon sous l'Occupation*, quoted in McIntosh, p. 147.

"Cuthbert is being tiresome . . .": Ibid., p. 118.

"If Cuthbert tiresome . . .": Ibid.

"You are really too well-known . . .": Buckmaster message to Virginia Hall, Oct. 6, 1943, Hall SOE Personnel File, HS 9/674/4, British Archives.

"When I came out here . . .": Virginia Hall letter to Buckmaster, SOE Hall Personnel File, HS 9/674/4, British Archives.

DIANE A.K.A. MARCELLE MONTAGNE (page 110)

"*WOLVES ARE AT* . . .": Pearson, Judith L. *The Wolves at the Door: The True Story of America's Greatest Female Spy*. Guilford, CT: Lyons Press, 2005. p. 188.

LA MADONE (page 120)

"Les marguerites fleuriront ce soir . . .": CIA.

"As long as Gévolde and Fayol were willing to do . . .": Virginia Hall OSS Activity Report, NARA, RG, 226, quoted in Purnell, p. 247.

"We know perfectly well just how much we owe her.": Fayol, *Le Chambon-sur-Lignon sous l'Occupation,* quoted in Fayol in rhapsodyinwords.com, Nov 20, 2019, "Remarkable Women."

VIRGINIA (page 134)

"extraordinary heroism in connection . . .": Distinguished Service Cross citation, The Hall of Valor Project.

"I don't want people to hear . . .": quoted by Hubert Petiet in Vincent Nouzille, *L'espionne: Virginia Hall, une Américaine dans la guerre.* Paris: Artheme Fayard, 2007, p. 14, quoted in Demetrios, p. 275.

"too many friends were killed because they talked too much.": Lorna Catling interview, Dec. 15, 2018 and *Nouzille, L'espionne: Virginia Hall, une Américaine dans la guerre.* Paris: Artheme Fayard, 2007, p. 5667.

DINDY (page 137)

"most original": *Quid Nunc*, p. 12, Mugele, p. 4.

"I must have liberty, . . .": *Quid Nunc*, p. 12. Quote based on Shakespeare's play *As You Like It,* Act II, Scene 7, Lines 48–49.

"Not bad for a girl from Baltimore": *Lorna Catling interview*, Dec. 15, 2018, *Not Bad for a Girl from Baltimore: The Story of Virginia Hall,* ee.usembassy.gov/wp-content/uploads/sites/207/Not-Bad-for-a-Girl-from-Baltimore.pdf.

Miss Virginia HALL - (34)

who works at the U.S. Embassy,
talked in my house last night of wanting to go for about a month to France
via Lisbon/Barcelona. In the latter
place she said her old chief would give
her a visa for France.

I did not press the question too
far at the time, although she talked also
of joining hands with the Quaker organisation as an excuse.

It strikes me that this lady, a
native of Baltimore, might well be used
for a mission and that we might :

a) facilitate her voyage to Lisbon
and back; and

b) stand her expenses while on her
trip in exchange for what service
she could render us.

I am getting fuller details on
her and will put her through the cards, at
the same time continuing approaches with
the same end in view.

MB

BIBLIOGRAPHY

Baltimore Sun. "Maryland Woman Is Driving Ambulance for French Army: Miss Virginia Hall Joined Allies Last February without Telling Family of Intentions," June 12, 1940.

———. "Virginia Goillot of French resistance, dies," July 13, 1982.

Barnard Archives and Special Collections. "Virginia Hall." Aug. 13, 2010. barnardarchives.wordpress.com/2010/08/13/virginia-hall/.

Binney, Marcus. *The Women Who Lived for Danger: The Women Agents of SOE in the Second World War.* London: Hodder & Stoughton, 2002.

British SOE. *How to Become a Spy: The World War II SOE Training Manual.* New York: Skyhorse Publishing, 2015.

Buckmaster, Maurice. *They Fought Alone: The Story of British Agents in France.* London: Odhams Press, 1958.

Burkett, Randy P. "Virginia Hall: OSS Hero, CIA Paramilitary Officer—Not a Victim." *Intelligencer: Journal of U.S. Intelligence Studies*, Summer–Fall 2019.

Carlomagno, Cameron. "Women in a Man's War: The Employment of Female Agents in the Special Operations Executive, 1940–1946." Master's thesis, Chapman University, 2019. doi.org/10.36837/chapman.000075.

Catling, Lorna. Interviewed by the author. Dec. 15, 2018; July 21, 2019; and June 2020.

Central Intelligence Agency. "The Debrief: Behind the Artifact—Virginia Hall." YouTube. Oct. 7, 2020. Video, 1:58. youtube.com/watch?v=t8qpwDUDz-c.

———. "Les Marguerites Fleuriront ce Soir." CIA. 2006. Video, 2:23. cia.gov/legacy/museum/artifact/les-marguerites-fleuriront-ce-soir/.

Churchill, Peter. *Duel of Wits.* New York: G. P. Putnam's Sons, 1953.

———. *Of Their Own Choice.* London: Hodder & Stoughton, 1952.

Cobb, Matthew. *The Resistance: The French Fight Against the Nazis.* London: Simon & Schuster UK, 2009.

Cowburn, Benjamin. *No Cloak, No Dagger.* London: Jarrolds, 1960.

Dalton, Hugh. *The Second World War Diary of Hugh Dalton 1940–1945.* London: Jonathan Cape, 1986.

Dear, Ian. *Sabotage and Subversion: The SOE and OSS at War.* London: Cassell Military Paperbacks, 1999.

de Vomécourt, Philippe. *An Army of Amateurs.* Garden City, NY: Doubleday, 1961.

———. *Who Lived to See the Day: France in Arms 1940–1945.* London: Hutchinson, 1961.

Demetrios, Heather. *Code Name Badass: The True Story of Virginia Hall.* New York: Atheneum, 2021.

Escott, Beryl E. *The Heroines of SOE: F Section: Britain's Secret Women in France.* Stroud, UK: History Press, 2014.

Fayol, Pierre. *Le Chambon-sur-Lignon sous l'occupation: Les résistances locales, l'aide interalliée, l'action de Virginia Hall (O.S.S.).* Paris: L'Harmattan, 1990.

———. "Remarkable Women: The Life and Times of Virginia Hall (Part 2)." *Rhap.so.dy in Words* (blog). Nov. 20, 2019. rhapsodyinwords.com/tag/pierre-fayol/.

Foot, M. R. D. *SOE: An Outline History of the Special Operations Executive, 1940–1946.* London: BBC, 1984.

———. *SOE in France.* London: Her Majesty's Stationery Office, 1966.

———. *SOE in France: An Account of the Work of the British Special Operations Executive in France, 1940–1944.* New York: Frank Cass Publishers, 2004.

Gordon, Bertram M., ed. *Historical Dictionary of WW II France: The Occupation, Vichy, and the Resistance, 1938–1946.* Westport, CT: Greenwood Press, 1998.

Gralley, Craig. "A Climb to Freedom: A Personal Journey in Virginia Hall's Steps." *Studies in Intelligence* 61, no.1 (Mar. 2017).

———. *Hall of Mirrors: Virginia Hall: America's Greatest Spy of World War II.* Pisgah Forest, NC: Chrysalis Books, 2019.

Grose, Peter. *A Good Place to Hide.* Boston: Nicholas Brealey Publishing, 2016.

Haines, Gerald K. "Virginia Hall Goillot: Career Intelligence Officer." *Prologue: Quarterly Journal of the National Archives,* Winter 1994.

Hall, Virginia. "France's Rabbits on Strike." *New York Post,* Jan. 22, 1942.

———. "Lyon—Odd Bits." *New York Post,* Jan. 13, 2018.

_____. "Vichy Bars Stock to Jews: Further Economic Bans expected." *New York Post,* Nov. 24, 1941.

———. "Vichy Exclusive: Bathroom Offices in Vichy: Reporter Finds Capital Crowded. Frenchmen Now Smoke Leaves." *New York Post,* Sept. 4, 1941.

Hall of Valor Project, The. "Virginia Hall." valor.militarytimes.com/hero/22199.

Into the Dark. Directed by Genevieve Simms. Imperial War Museum Short Film Festival, 2005. Video, 16:35. vimeo.com/33965059.

Laneri, Raquel. "She was a Post columnist—and a heroic WWII spy." *New York Post,* Jan. 13, 2018. nypost.com/2018/01/13/she-was-a-post-columnist-and-a-heroic-wwii-spy/.

Langelaan, George. *Knights of the Floating Silk.* London: Hutchinson, 1959.

Mackenzie, William. *The Secret History of the SOE: The Special Operations Executive 1940–1945.* London: St Ermin's Press, 2002.

McIntosh, Elizabeth P. *Sisterhood of Spies: The Women of the OSS.* New York: Dell Publishing, 1998.

Mitchell, Don. *The Lady Is a Spy: Virginia Hall, World War II Hero of the French Resistance*. New York: Scholastic, 2019.

Moorehead, Caroline. *Village of Secrets: Defying the Nazis in Vichy France*. New York: Harper, 2014.

Mugele, Nancy. "The Lady Who Limps." *Connections* (Roland Park Country School Alumnae Magazine), Spring 2007.

Pearson, Judith L. *The Wolves at the Door: The True Story of America's Greatest Female Spy*. Guilford, CT: Lyons Press, 2005.

Purnell, Sonia. *A Woman of No Importance: The Untold Story of the American Spy Who Helped Win World War II*. New York: Viking, 2019.

———. "Virginia Hall Was America's Most Successful Female WWII Spy. But She Was Almost Kept from Serving." *Time*, April 9, 2019. time.com/5566062/virginia-hall/.ff.

Quid Nunc, Graduating Class of 1924 Yearbook, Roland Park Country School Archives.

Richards, Sir Brooks. "SOE and Sea Communications." In *Special Operations Executive: A New Instrument of War*, edited by Mark Seaman. London and New York: Routledge, 2006.

Rosbottom, Ronald C. *When Paris Went Dark: The City of Light Under German Occupation, 1940–1944*. New York: Little, Brown and Company, 2014.

Rossiter, Margaret. *Women in the Resistance*. New York: Praeger, 1986.

Ruby, Marcel. *F Section, SOE: The Buckmaster Networks*. London: Leo Cooper, 1988.

Simpson, William. *I Burned My Fingers*. London: Putnam, 1955.

United States Holocaust Memorial Museum. *Women in World War II: The Spies They Never Saw Coming*. Facebook Live Series. Mar. 10, 2021. Video, 45:00. facebook.com/holocaustmuseum/videos/women-in-world-war-ii-the-spies-they-never-saw-coming/292493155623874.

Vigurs, Kate. *Mission France: The True History of the Women of SOE*. New Haven: Yale University Press, 2021.

PICTURE CREDITS

ABOUT THE AUTHOR

Claudia Friddell, the author of 8 narrative nonfiction books, loves writing true stories that highlight extraordinary people and events from America's past. She most especially loves writing books about heroic women like Virginia Hall who are timeless role models for readers of all ages, including *Grace Banker and Her Hello Girls Answer the Call* and *To the Front! Clara Barton Braves the Battle of Antietam*. A former teacher, Claudia is inspired by the students, educators, history buffs, and avid readers who she meets at author events across the country. She and her husband have two grown children and live in Maryland. Visit her and some of her favorite Americans at claudiafriddell.com.

MEET CLAUDIA FRIDDELL'S OTHER WARTIME HEROES

Eureka Silver Honor Award, California Reading Association

NCSS Notable Trade Book

Kansas NEA Reading Circle Recommended Title

Texas Topaz Nonfiction Reading list

Septima Clark Women in Literature Honor Award

NCSS Notable Trade Book

Bank Street Best Books List (Outstanding Merit)

ALA Rise: A Feminist Book Project List